SPAIN AGAIN

BY ALVAH BESSIE

Novels:
The Symbol
The un-Americans
Bread & a Stone
Dwell in the Wilderness
One for My Baby (in process)
The Serpent Was More Subtil (in process)

Autobiography:
Spain Again
Inquisition in Eden
Men in Battle

Anthology:
The Heart of Spain (editor)

SPAIN AGAIN

ALVAH BESSIE

CHANDLER & SHARP PUBLISHERS, INC.

SAN FRANCISCO

Acknowledgment is made to the following authors and publishers for their gracious permission to quote from the following books and scripts:

Pandora Films, S.A. (Madrid), screenplay, *España Otra Vez* by Jaime Camino and Román Gubern, with the collaboration of Alvah Bessie; Harcourt, Brace & Co., *In Place of Splendor*, by Constancia de la Mora; Grove Press, *La Guerre Est Finie*, screenplay by Jorge Semprun; Editions Seghers (Paris), *Mourir à Madrid*, texte de Madeleine Chapsal; Les Editeurs Français Réunis (Paris), *Virage Sur l'Aile*, par Ignacio Hidalgo de Cisnéros; Colección Ebro (Paris), *Nuestra Guerra*, par Enrique Lister.

The photograph on page 6 was taken in 1938 by an itinerant photographer. The photograph on page 159 was taken by VALB veteran Mike Ehrenburg, and is reproduced here with his permission. The photograph on page 160 was taken by Steve Troxil (VALB), and is reproduced here with his permission. All other photographs, including that used on the cover, are the work of Martha G. Frias.

The map appearing on page 206 is from *Dreams and Nightmares* — a documentary film by Abe Osheroff (VALB), 1974, and is reproduced here with the permission of Mr. Osheroff.

Bessie, Alvah Cecil, 1904-
    Spain again.

    Autobiographical.
    1. Bessie, Alvah Cecil, 1904-   —Journeys—Spain. 2. España otra vez.
[Motion picture] I. Title.
PS3503.E778Z52   813'.5'2 [B]   74-28742
ISBN 0-88316-516-3

Book designed by Joseph M. Roter

a Jaime

Alamedas de mi sangre.
¡Alto dolor de olmos negros!
¿Qué nuevos vientos lleváis?
¿Qué murmuran vuestros ecos?
¿Qué apretáis en mi garganta
que siento el tallo del hielo
aún más frío que la muerte
estrangular mi deseo?
¿Qué agudo clamor de angustia
rueda corazón adentro
golpe a golpe retumbando
como campana de duelo . . .

Emilio Prados

CONTENTS

SPAIN AGAIN

I

"This passport is not valid . . ."

1

It began with a conversation in October 1964. I had been employed (temporarily, again) by a monster in San Francisco who was permitted by his father to run six movie houses and had invented an international film festival all by himself.

The word monster is used advisedly, for I was the seventh person in three years to hold the job of public relations man for this character, whose only claim to fame was an anachronistic Royal Air Force mustache (no pilot he) with a wingspread of seven inches.

Why his disguise (which disguised nothing) infuriated instead of amused me I do not know. I had not been infuriated over 40 years earlier by the fact that Professor Spiers of Columbia College had grown the mustache and goatee of The Three Musketeers. In fact, I was entirely sympathetic to his personal tragedy: apparently he had wanted to be a Frenchman, and every gesture, every expression of his face, even when he was speaking English, was totally and authentically Gallic.

A public relations man is not supposed to have opinions about the product he publicizes. Or, if he has such opinions he should have the good grace to keep them to himself instead of running around from movie critics to Sunday magazine editors, saying, "Here are some pix from the latest turd we're showing," or, "This thing opens Friday. Send your second-string, or skip it."

But when I found myself not only handling the six movie houses *and* the man's personal film festival (no extra pay but lots of extra hours) my tendency toward instant choler reached a nodal point.

I had also noticed among the entries a film from Franco Spain that would be accompanied by its director, and I was prepared to hate that man on sight. I was prepared to hate him because I was an unreconstructed character myself who—26 years earlier—had fought as an infantryman against the regime that he and his film theoretically represented.

The man I met in the Jack Tar Hotel a couple days before the festival opened was 28 years old. He was small in stature, wore a thick mustache and a pair of bedroom eyes. He even had dimples and he was extremely charming, which made me even more suspicious. And why not? If you are an accredited representative of such a regime, a regime that is loathed throughout the world except in the seats of real power in the "free" world, you have an obligation to be something more than pleasant.

Since he could not speak more than a few words of English and since his French, while fluent, was even more unintelligible than mine, which was not fluent at all, I attempted to resurrect my illiterate Spanish, a language I had picked up between frontline actions in 1938. Most of it consisted of such pragmatic phrases as: "I'm wounded," "It hurts very much," "Left leg," "Where's the toilet?," "How much?," "I'm hungry," "In the balls."

Being a gentleman as well as a Spanish fascist (you simply do not get out of Spain unless you are *persona grata*, my unreconstructed mind informed me), the young man who was exhibiting his first feature film in competition asked me politely where I had learned his language.

● I never learned it at all. And I don't think you'd be very pleased to know of the circumstances under which I learned what little I learned. (Vehemently; even angrily) I learned it *in Spain*!

● When was that?

● (With considerable hostility)—In 1938!

● (Pause)—1938? (Another pause, finally looking up from the floor of the hotel room, which he had been inspecting with more than ordinary interest)—The Lincoln Battalion?

*

Actually, *that's* when it all began, in 1938 in fact, while I was sitting under a hazel-bush one night in June with a man 24 years old. I was 34 and his adjutant; he was my company commander. His name was Aaron Lopoff.

There was a moon that night and we had been talking about totally innocuous things, such as the problem he had retaining me as his adjutant when our battalion commander, Milton Wolff, was insisting that he get a Spanish adjutant. We had been talking about the problem of getting real tobacco to smoke, instead of *avellano* leaves, about the food, which had deteriorated greatly since Franco's spring offensive had cut Spain in half.

Then, suddenly, Aaron said, "You started something when you joined the International Brigade, Papa."

The remark seemed commonplace to me and my interpretation of it was equally commonplace: what he was trying to say was that I stood little chance of getting out of Spain alive. We knew the war was lost, even then. We had known it since the April retreats had cut Spain in two and Franco reached the Mediterranean at Tortosa. We had known it since our ranks had been decimated and then been filled again with Spanish *reclutas*, many of whom were even too young to shave.

But Aaron was a better prophet for himself than he was for me: he got a machine-gun bullet through his head one night that August after we had crossed the Ebro River in the greatest, and last, offensive the Republic mounted. We had

AARON (left): "You started something ... Papa ..."

launched a night attack from the top of Hill 666 in the Sierra Pandols overlooking Gandesa.

Evacuated, Aaron was sent first to a hospital near Barcelona, in Mataró, I believe; then, because facilities were lacking to treat a wound that had destroyed one eye and sparked a meningitic infection, they started to move him toward France. He died en route. For more than 25 years I had kept a slip of paper on which I had written: "Aaron. Town cemetery. Santa Coloma de las Planes (Gerona prov.)." I do not know who gave me that piece of information, or when.

Of course, Aaron had meant something quite different that night under the *avellano* bush, but it took me 12 years to realize what it was, and by then I was in a Federal prison in Texas.

*

Who can say when any event originates or how any process is initiated? Did it begin when the *Brooklyn Sunday Eagle* sent me out to interview André Malraux in 1937? He had come to the States on a speaking tour and appeared in his Spanish Republican Air Force uniform and rich and poor alike poured money into medical aid for Spain. He had fascinated me, not only because of what he represented, not only because of his novel, *La Condition Humaine* (*Man's Fate*), but also because he was the only human being I had ever met who could speak and exhale simultaneously through both nostrils. (People said he was a dope fiend. People told me later that in Spain he had been an agent of France's *Deuxième Bureau*, but I never believed it even when he became a PR man for General de Gaulle.)

Did it begin when—inspired romantically by Malraux himself—and finally realizing a dream that was born in 1909 when I saw Wilbur Wright fly around Manhattan Island, I started to take flying lessons from a young man who had recently returned from Spain himself? (No—I remember now—I was taking flying lessons before Malraux arrived.)

Was it advanced further because while learning to fly I had met a famous racing and test pilot whom I brought home for dinner—and who stayed three weeks? And because, when he finally left, my wife of seven years and the mother of my two sons announced that she had fallen in love with the man?

Had it originated in the fact that I had married this fine young woman when I was 26 and she was 32 and I, being a cynical young man, did not believe in love? (One day in 1932 she called me from Oyster Bay and said, "I'm sick of this affair. Come out tomorrow and marry me or to hell with you.")

Did it start when I not only walked out of our home on Joralemon Street but also quit the *Eagle* to write publicity for the Spanish Republic, and then was fired and decided to go to Spain myself?

Or had it all begun much earlier because I was repelled by everything my father represented (he was a stock broker and manufacturer) and my older brother accepted his word as Gospel? I had refused to become a lawyer or a business man, and I walked around the Columbia campus wearing a Windsor tie and writing bad poetry while my brother went on to become the successful physician and surgeon my father had suggested he become.

Shall we get Freudian about it or shall we apply the Marxian dialectic that says, in effect, that you are what you *do*? ("It is not the consciousness of men that determines their being, but, on the contrary, their social being that determines their consciousness.") Or shall we cook up a mixture of the two to explain why one son of a conservative Republican becomes a conservative Republican while the younger son becomes a radical?

2

Whatever the origin of the fact, the ramifications of theory and practice or the interpenetrations of opposites (courage *vs.* fear, comfort *vs.* danger, escape *vs.* commitment, romanticism *vs.* a realistic appraisal of the forces involved), Spain became the focus of my life, the zenith and the nadir, the past, the present and the future.

It affected everything that has happened to me since: it was as though I had been walking down a straight road and suddenly (almost inadvertently) had executed a 90-degree turn—to the left. It was responsible for the fact that my by-line no longer appeared in "respectable" periodicals but became acceptable to the radical. It forced me to become a drama, film and book critic for *New Masses*, since nobody else in New York would hire me. It brought me before the House Committee on Un-American Activities in 1947, after a thoroughly incredible interlude in Lotosland as a screenwriter, and it locked me in a prison cell in Texas when I refused to testify before that committee about my political beliefs and affiliations.

It accounts for the fact that after prison I was doubly unemployable by the respectable media and wound up for five years in the International office of Harry Bridges' longshoremen's and warehousemen's union. After that I was *triply* unemployable until a nightclub owner in San Francisco thought it would be cute to use me as a stage manager, light man and off-stage announcer for seven years: what the hell, it only cost him $85 to $105 a week (the union minimum was $150) and he could tell his more important customers that he had a notorious character behind the scenes.

It influenced almost every review of every book I have written since 1939. It even accounts for my employment by the monstrous director of the film festival—for there was nobody else in town who would work for *him*. And on the positive side it may even explain the fact that my only happy marriage was contracted with a French woman of total Spanish ancestry (Andalucía-Murcia-Alicante).

It is scarcely my fault that the passage of decades has not dimmed my almost total recall of sights and sounds: the white and blinding summer sun of Spain, the bone-chilling *mistral* and the freezing rain, the snatches of conversation, song and music, the smell of sage and ripe grapes and tuns of olive oil, and oranges and rotten figs and rotting bodies.

I do not even have to close my eyes to see the outlines of cork and olive trees, the ancient, writhing vines bare in winter, the square houses built of flat stones and adobe, the red tile roofs, the black clothing of the peasant women and the *peto* worn by the older men to keep their bellies warm, the weather-beaten faces like ruined walls and the young boys with the soft skin and black eyes of the most beautiful young girls in the world, the jagged rocks rising beside the highway outside Pinell-de-Bray in Catalonia where—I am certain —there is still a burro path that leads to the peak we called Hill 666 where the American volunteers suffered their greatest agony between August 15th and August 27th of 1938.

No day has passed since July 18, 1936, that has not found me scanning the daily papers for news of Spain; few books that have been published in English, French or Spanish have escaped reading. Instant outrage has been evoked a thousand times by the attempts, not only by outright fascists but by liberal Cold Warriors who think of themselves as a Loyal Opposition, to rewrite the history of that little war that left a million Spanish dead and has never ended for a moment since *El Generalisimo* Franco followed his victorious Moors (at a safe distance) into a Madrid that had not fallen in almost three years of most unequal combat.

For if you discount the memoirs written by his propagandists, who tell us with straight faces that the vast majority of the Spanish people supported The Most General and that Guernica was destroyed by "the Reds" and not by Hitler's Condor Legion, you still have to deal with the more subtle liars who have been busy cleaning their noses for decades.

They will admit generously that the Spanish war was a "just" cause, *but*:

(1) The Republic was weak and vacillating;

(2) The confusion that obtained during the war was the product of rival Spanish ideologies of right, left and center;

(3) The devil-in-the-cheese was the Spanish Communist Party that lusted for power, sabotaged everything in sight and murdered its enemies wholesale;

(4) The biggest devil-in-the-cheese was of course the Soviet Union, which *wanted* the Republic to lose for its own nefarious reasons and guaranteed its defeat by withdrawing its support. (Corollary: The Soviet Union also "stole" the Republic's gold reserve, which had been sent there for safekeeping.)

Of course, these revisionists will not tell you that the *only* major support in terms of arms, money and international solidarity the Republic could command was Soviet support; they will not admit that the weakness and vacillation of the Republic stemmed from the ruthless sabotage of its aims and its reforms by internal enemies who started in 1931 to conspire with Hitler and Mussolini to overthrow it legally, if possible; if not, by force of arms.

On the one hand they blame the Communist Party of Spain for misleading the people (it misled them so effectively that the Party grew from 30,000 members to over 300,000 during the course of the war); then they reverse their field and say the Party should have carried through a socialist revolution

(as the Trotskyist P.O.U.M.* advocated) instead of offering
its wholehearted support to the Republic.**

For there are no more flaming revolutionaries alive than
the Establishment's Loyal Opposition who told us, in our own
time and in our own country, that the war in Vietnam was
illegal and immoral—but we could not withdraw. They also
tell us that black Americans deserve a better break but it is
wrong for them to "riot" in the streets out of their bottomless
desperation because law and order must be maintained.

No rewrite of history, no matter how ingenious or how
cynical, can ever negate the fact that the majority of the
world's people immediately understood the Spanish war for
exactly what it was: a pure and simple and heartbreakingly
courageous struggle by the people of Spain to prevent their
country from being thrust backward into the Middle Ages.
That is why they lent it whatever support they could.

No amount of lying by the late egomaniacal Johnson,
Dean Rusk, the Joint Chiefs of Staff, the press and radio and
television, the bankrupt General Westmoreland or any of their
henchmen, high or low, obscured the fact that Vietnam, with
significant differences, was a replay of Spain with the dis-

---

* Workers Party of Marxist Unification.

** "It is plain that the principal causes of our defeat were: the participation of the
armed forces of Germany and Italy on the side of the insurrectionists; the complicity
of the rulers of England, France and the United States with Italy and fascist Germany
in strangling the Spanish Republic; the persistent negative activities of the Non-
Intervention Committee; the closing of the French frontier and a whole series of other
international plots against the Spanish people. But all this, which is established,
should not serve as a smoke screen to conceal the military and political errors committed by us throughout the war, and which contributed to our defeat. I will refer to
certain of these." Enrique Lister, Commanding General, Vth Army Corps, in the
Introduction to his *Nuestra Guerra*. Paris: Coleccion Ebro, 1966 — *Translation,
A.B.*

United States in the role of Hitler and Mussolini.* That is why the majority of the people of the world opposed the American "posture" in Indochina and were not deceived by our pretensions.

3

"You may not think my film is very sensational," said the little man from Barcelona the night it was shown at the San Francisco Film Festival. "But you have to understand that —for my country—it represents something a little revolutionary."

I smiled. "And what is that?"

"This is the first time, in a film made in Spain, that it has been admitted that a married woman will sometimes step outside her marriage and commit adultery."

He was right. Since adultery (as well as mindless violence) has been the hallmark of the American film ever since World War II, the San Francisco critics did not care too much for his picture. They admitted that it was well-directed, well-acted and beautifully photographed, but it seemed commonplace to them.

---

* "Indiscriminate genocidal bombing attacks and search-and-destroy missions are not undertaken to preserve the freedom of the Vietnamese people nor to protect them from China. These acts are coldly calculated to secure an American *place d'armes* on the continent of Asia, just as the fascist crusade against the Spanish Republicans was intended to secure a base of operations for the greater war already on the planning boards of the general staffs in Berlin and Rome. To what other end do vast permanent encampments arise at Camranh Bay and in Thailand?" Robert Colodny, *Spain & Vietnam.* New York: Veterans of the Abraham Lincoln Brigade, 1967.

Part of their reaction to the film might have stemmed from the fact that the festival itself was such a howling fiasco that anything exhibited took second place to the ball they were having with the event itself.

The Director never ran another festival and the little man from Spain went home again, but I imagine he had some fun before he left: he was captured by a sensationally built Finnish free-lance photographer who had shown up suddenly at the Gala Awards Banquet & Ball complete with cameras and the lowest-cut gown I have ever seen outside a whorehouse. She spotted his bushy mustache and his bedroom eyes the moment she entered the grand ballroom of the Sheraton-Palace Hotel. ("A kiss without a mustache," says an old Spanish proverb, "is like an egg without salt.")

4

The festival ended on a Tuesday night. On Friday morning, after a considerate lapse of three days, The Director fired me without notice.

On the strength of this magnificent job with the festival (and the six theaters), my wife and I had purchased a brand-new 1965 Mustang—two weeks before I was fired. There now ensued another period of unemployment, broken only by a small job that lasted four weeks, publicizing the only motion picture house in San Francisco that consistently shows good films (mostly foreign) but cannot afford a full-time PR man.

To make the cheese more binding, my wife, who had worked for seven years as a multilingual secretary for a worldwide corporation, was suddenly discharged. (No reason given.)

Great corporations, however (contrary to my unreconstructed hatred for their guts), are sometimes far more generous and just than individual entrepreneurs who live on the bounty of their fathers. Therefore, we started to live carefully on her retirement and severance pay and she, being a practical woman (whom I sometimes call *Madame la Caisse* when I grow momentarily angry at her practicality), asked the State of California for retraining benefits. She had heard that court reporters (stenotypists) make a lot of money and she started to go to school to learn this formidable discipline.

We will draw the curtain at this point while we both collect our "benefits" and she goes quietly mad trying to master the stenotype machine and I go loudly mad trying to put up with her suddenly altered disposition *and* write a novel at the same time. (Students of psychology may be interested in the fact that when my wife is angry she swears in French. When she is *very* angry she swears in Spanish. But when she is *really* angry she swears in Arabic. This may have something to do with the fact that she was a French citizen, born of Spanish parents in Algeria, and brought up in Morocco.)

5

A discreet Christmas card in Spanish arrived that December (1964) with no return address on the envelope nor any signature inside except a single initial. Emboldened by what seemed to me a tentative and pitiful cry for help, I wrote a one-page letter to the address the man with the dimples had provided before his departure from San Francisco.

In due course a reply arrived—in French: "I liked very much what I was able to learn of your country. If there are problems still to be resolved there, I can see that your people are very young and will, with time, be able to achieve new conquests in the realm of liberty. This is my hope."

The man was only 28 years old and although he bore himself with the demeanor of a thoroughly mature individual, I doubted that he had reached such a peak of maturity (from Mt. Tibidabo, perhaps, which lies behind Barcelona?) that he could condescend in this manner to our adolescent nation.

He said he was sorry we had not been able to talk more while he was in town. He said he was preparing a new film, a comedy he expected to shoot in March. He remarked cryptically that while it was a comedy, "I nevertheless pose the problem of the necessity for adventure and action in order to emerge from the passive life which is ours here in Spain." (Now, surely, *that* was a *de profundis clamavi*, or was it?)

Then came a vertiginous statement, delivered in a deceptively calm tone of voice:

"I was very 'touched' (why the quotation marks?) by the reading of your book translated into Spanish. You must believe me when I say that, so far as I was concerned, it is one of the most moving books I have ever read. I read it in three days, so involved was I in the plot of this lucid and impassioned document. . . . Others would certainly enjoy the dialectic of your novel. I find that the greatest value of the book lies in the fact that it creates a unity between history, document and the interior struggle of the characters, forming at one and the same time an objective and poignant piece of testimony. . . ."

FLASHBACK: The only novel of mine that had ever been translated into Spanish had been published in Argentina in 1957 and was originally titled *The un-Americans*. Its Spanish title was even more likely to appeal to Latin Americans who live in fear and hatred of The Colossus of the North: *Los Antinorteamericanos*.

According to its Argentine publisher only 4,000 copies

were ever printed, although, paradoxically, I had been told by friends who travel in the Southern hemisphere that it was a "best seller" in every South American country, including Mexico and Cuba.

Early in 1966 its publisher suddenly announced the forthcoming translation and publication of one of my other books, *Inquisition in Eden*—without benefit of any contract whatsoever. I complained about this and he sent the contract. I delayed signing it and, in July, I received an unsigned letter from him:

". . . One of the first measures of the military government was to attack the credit cooperatives. . . . Well, we depend almost totally on the credit extended to us by these cooperatives. The sudden disappearance of the said credit and the almost total drop in sales in bookstores frightened by [the recent *coup d'état*] have prevented us from continuing our editorial activities."

Naturally, I immediately wrote to him at his home address, and just as naturally, I never received an answer. All sorts of roundabout inquiries were initiated by me, by my New York agent through a firm in Buenos Aires that had formerly acted as *his* agent. All were fruitless.

The first strange by-product of this shadow play (which occurred almost two years before the military *coup* in Argentina) was the unexpected announcement that the man I had met in San Francisco had somehow found a copy of my book in Spain. How did it get there? Was there an underground apparatus that shipped anti-Franco (pro-Loyalist) material into the private domain of The Most General? Did it circulate secretly? In how many copies? How had this particular man found this book? How many other people there had found and read it?

I wrote to the man with the bedroom eyes, hinting at my

curiosity (and my unemployment), and suggesting, as a joke, that he might want to hire me as an assistant director. He replied.

He did not refer to the novel again but he took my joke seriously and explained that it would be very difficult for me to collaborate with him. "For an American, the salaries paid here would seem very small ($80 a week), and it is not easy for a foreigner to work on a Spanish production. I suppose you will understand these and other obvious reasons."

He must have thought I was an idiot, so I hastened to explain that I was not and that the request had been a joke, although $80 a week was $80 more a week than I was earning. There was no reply—for 11 months.

In December of 1965 there arrived a handsome calendar for 1966, imprinted with the name of a moving-picture company in Barcelona (*Tibidabo Films*), and containing reproductions in color of some of the finest paintings in the Prado of Madrid. We wrote and thanked the little man and sent a Christmas card in turn. There was no answer.

There was silence throughout 1966 although one odd communication came to me from a publishing house in Barcelona. It enclosed a page from a catalogue issued by a wholesale bookseller in Buenos Aires, announcing the publication—by my vanished publisher—of a book called *Maccarthysmo en Hollywood—Bessie, Alvah*. . . The publisher in Barcelona requested three copies of the original book (*Inquisition in Eden*), two "for reading and one for submission to the censor," as well as rights of translation and publication into Castilian Spanish and Catalan!

My first impulse, immediately suppressed, was to write a letter saying, "What *are* you, some kind of a nut?" I told my New York agent about this and she suggested we send the three copies. I suggested firmly that we send *no* copies inasmuch as there was not a chance in the world that an anti-

Franco book, a radical book, would survive a first reading in the publisher's office, let alone the *Censura* in Madrid. She sent one copy anyhow. There was no answer.

At the end of 1966 a simple Christmas card arrived informing us that our little man had finished shooting his second feature film. *"Es una comedia muy bonita,"* he wrote. We answered with a long letter letter on 1 January 1967 to which there was no reply whatsoever.

To hell with *him*, I thought. What does he think I am, some kind—?

Premonitory thunder was heard early in 1967. A magazine editor in New York suddenly wrote saying he had recently seen a friend of mine I had not met in over 15 years. This friend had recently been in Madrid where he had learned that "the hottest underground book in Spain—I kid you not —is . . . *Los Antinorteamericanos!*"

I wrote my long-lost friend in New York and said, "How come?" I asked innumerable questions. I wanted to know how he had learned about this, how the book was circulated, whether it was the Argentine edition or had been pirated in Spain, how extensively it had been read, had he seen a copy of it and did he know how I could lay my hands on one?

His reply was slow in coming and I had large visions, *not* of large royalties, underground or openly arrived at, but of my novel working quietly and effectively to subvert the regime of The Most General and contribute—in its small and modest way—to his eventual downfall.

Was it not a true picture of certain aspects of the Spanish war (as well as the drive toward conformity in the U.S.A.)? Was not its "dialectic" fascinating? Did it not create a unity between history, document and the interior struggle of the characters, forming at one and the same time an objective and poignant piece of testimony? Had it not been a resounding failure in my own country—viciously attacked when not sedulously ignored—thereby *proving* its validity?

In her farewell speech to the departing International Brigades in Barcelona, Dolores Ibárruri (*La Pasionaría*) had said: "We shall not forget you, and when the olive tree of peace puts forth its leaves again, entwined with the laurels of the Spanish Republic's victory—come back! . . . Come back to us. With us those of you who have no country will find one, those of you who have lived deprived of friendship will find friends, and all of you will find the love and gratitude of the whole Spanish people. . . ." (That implied promise of honorary citizenship began to look more promising.)

When my friend finally replied, he merely said that he had met a motion-picture director and a producer in Madrid, both of whom had read my novel and thought highly of it. How extensively it was circulated he did not know, but he gave me both these names (entirely strange to me) and suggested I write to either one, "and you will get an answer because they both admire you and the book."

Of course, I wrote immediately—and most discreetly raised my questions. Of course, I never received an answer.

6

Then the lightning struck. A letter dated 26 September 1967 calmly set forth a proposition that simply could not be made. A Spanish film company, said the man with dimples, on his insistence wished me to come to Barcelona "immediately," all expenses paid.

"I am writing a new screenplay," said the letter, "which concerns a person, a former fighter in the Spanish Civil War who served on the Republican side as a doctor. This person is an American and he returns to Spain to attend a medical congress (he is a neurosurgeon). This is an extremely moving experience for him, to find himself once more in Barcelona after 30 years of absence. When the congress is over, he returns to the United States.

"The plot is much more complex and revolves around his discovery of the reality of the country today, as contrasted with his nostalgia concerning the period of the war.

"I believe this is a moving theme that will surely interest you. Therefore, I raise the question of your collaboration with me. . . ."

He had raised a hell of a lot of questions beyond my possible collaboration. He had raised the ghost of the fact that I had been blacklisted in the motion picture industry in my own country for 20 solid years—and here I was being offered an opportunity to work once more at a craft I thoroughly enjoy.

He was naively (?) summoning to Spain a man who had been the enemy of its regime for more than 30 years; who had written and spoken against it indefatigably; who had agreed that very week to make another speech, commemorating the 30th anniversary of the International Brigades, from the pulpit of a church in Los Angeles and who was writing—when his letter was received—as violent an attack on Spanish fascism as he had ever managed to achieve.

He had raised unanswerable questions, but since *he* had raised them, I decided to restate them in another form:

". . . What will you be saying in this film? Will you be able to say it? The American doctor appeals to me enormously; I understand what he felt when he returned to Spain. . . . How does his attitude change? *Does* his attitude change by the time he returns to the United States? What does he feel about what he did in Spain 30 years before?"

Naively, I expected answers to these questions and I received a reply two weeks later which answered none of them. He apologized for the fact that beyond my transportation both ways and a daily stipend of 1,000 pesetas (then worth about $16), his producing company could not afford to pay me what I was worth—as a screenwriter. (There was a time when I was "worth" $600 a week. Now I was worth exactly nothing.)

He said he could not "go into details" about the story beyond what he had told me, but he added the following details: ". . . On his return to Barcelona all his memories are stirred again and he looks for María, his sweetheart of that (earlier) time. Instead of finding María, he finds her daughter, Fascination. But the relationship can have no possible future. He returns to the U.S.A." (*Aha*! my unreconstructed mind said, out loud, a crappy love story that bilks all the issues and says nothing.)

He wanted to know, in the event that I decided to come (and I had told him I would not come without my wife and hinted delicately that *her* way ought to be paid, too), whether he should send me an "open" ticket or would I prefer to be reimbursed when I arrived? (He said nothing about my wife.) He thought perhaps I could also help him obtain the services of a good actor for the leading role, someone like William Holden, Henry Fonda, James Mason or Yves Montand. His company would agree to pay such an actor the sum of—$30,000.

What do you do in such a case, laugh or cry? Thirty thousand dollars for Henry Fonda? For Yves Montand? Collaboration on a full-length screenplay in a period of three weeks—the time he said I would be needed?

What I did, without talking to my wife more than five minutes, was to send a cable: SEND ONE ROUNDTRIP TICKET VIA AIRFRANCE SAN FRANCISCO OFFICE. LETTER FOLLOWS.

The letter that followed said we had both applied for renewal of our passports. It said my wife would follow in a week or two. It urged him not to buy me a 30-day "excursion" ticket since my wife and I intended to grasp the opportunity offered and travel a little in France and Morocco after the job in Spain was done. It said he could not hope to get an actor of the caliber or reputation of William Holden or even James Mason for $30,000. It did *not* say anything about what was going on inside a man who might return to Spain after a period of 29 years, to a Spain he deeply loved but which was still dominated by the Spanish butcher who was maintained in power *only* by the money, arms and bases his own country had supplied and was supplying.

What was going on inside the man was nothing short of instant schizophrenia. His mind and his emotions were traveling at jet velocity while his body remained rooted. He was thinking of himself alternately as an international *agent provocateur*—and as a fink. He had scornfully berated several other veterans of the Spanish war for returning to the scene of the crime, as well as any number of friends who had bolstered the regime with hard-earned American tourist dollars.

He remembered that the first time he had gone to Spain his passport had been stamped NOT VALID FOR TRAVEL IN SPAIN. Well, in 1938 he had not *used* the passport for such a purpose. He had used it to go to France, and from there he had climbed the Pyrenees mountains with several hundred other foreigners one January night to get into Spain. So far as the U.S. Department of State was concerned, this was apparently a distinction without a difference, for it had promptly lifted the passport on his return to the United States and would not give it back.

As a matter of fact, he had not applied for a passport again until 1961, not only because he had had no money to travel but also because—for several years—the passport application had carried a non-Communist oath and he was damned if he would sign any oath for *any* government swearing that he was or was not a this-and-that or believed so-and-so or did not believe it, or did or did not associate with whomsoever.

When, in 1961, he had obtained another passport because he had been invited (expenses paid) to attend a 25th anniversary commemoration of the International Brigade in East Berlin, there had been no such oath but a paragraph required that he state in writing: "In 1938 I served in the International Brigade, which was part of the Spanish Republican (Loyalist) Army. I did not take an oath of allegiance to the Spanish government, nor vote in any election."

That passport had been stamped "not valid" for travel to or in Communist-controlled portions of China, Korea, Vietnam, Albania and Cuba. It had *not* been stamped not valid for travel in the German Democratic Republic because that nation of 17,000,000 people, which was established in 1949, simply did not exist so far as the Department of State was concerned. (It exists now.) The trip itself he had romantically regarded as a reward for virtue.

In 1965 virtue had been rewarded again by another invitation to Berlin and Weimar to attend an international writers' congress, but the State Department had been having conniption fits over an American who had fought with Fidel Castro, and it had taken the intervention of an attorney (as well as still another U.S. Supreme Court decision in a related case) to pry the passport out of the hot little hands of the ineffable lady who ruled that division of the Department.

We had applied for renewal of our passports right after the 29 September letter had arrived. I told my wife that mine would not be renewed and she laughed at me. Her passport came 48 hours later. I laughed at *her*. But she had the last laugh for mine came five days later. (For some mysterious reason, Albania could now be visited but two other prohibited nations had emerged—the Syrian Arab Republic and the

United Arab Republic—making a total of six countries off limits for Americans. A small world and getting smaller.)

No ticket had come from Barcelona. Instead, a mysterious cable in Spanish arrived saying: MONDAY 23 [October] YOU WILL RECEIVE TELEGRAM CONFIRMING SENDING TICKET AIRFRANCE. (It was from Madrid.)

The 23rd came and went and on the 24th *I* sent a cable to Barcelona: HAVE NOT RECEIVED TELEGRAM OR TICKET. PLEASE ADVISE SOON.

At 8 a.m. the 25th another cable came from Madrid, reading: TODAY IN YOUR NAME TICKET AIR-FRANCE ADVISE ME ARRIVAL BARCELONA.

Then the schizophrenia began to get out of hand and it was not only mine. At 9 a.m. the same day TWA called to inform me that it had a ticket for me from San Francisco to—Madrid. I told TWA that I was expecting a ticket all right, but not to Madrid, to Barcelona, and not from TWA but from Air France. TWA's lady was most diplomatic and said she would query Air France in my behalf.

At 9:30 a.m. Air France called and said *it* had a ticket for me. No, the Air France lady had not heard from the TWA lady. Yes, the ticket was to Barcelona. The ticket had not been purchased by the little man's moving-picture company in Barcelona, which was called *Tibidabo Films*, but by a motion-picture company in Madrid called *Pandora Films*. Also, it was not an "open" ticket; it was not even a 30-day excursion ticket. It was a 21-day excursion ticket which, of course, could be exchanged in Barcelona for an open ticket on payment of an additional $205.60.

Pandora indeed!

The Air France lady informed us that the connecting flight from Paris to Barcelona would be made aboard an *Iberia* plane and we cabled the information that we would arrive together the 31st of October on IB Flight #191. (We didn't, but that part of the story comes later, if at all.)

For now the schizophrenia *really* took over—not *Iberia*'s, not *Pandora*'s, not *Tibidabo*'s, not TWA's or Air France's, but my very own:

I suddenly remembered the rumor that all the records of the International Brigades had been captured when Barcelona fell to the fascists in 1939. The very address of the I. B. office popped into my mind: Pasaje Mendez Vigo #5.

I wondered why I had just reviewed a new book—*not* for the *San Francisco Chronicle* (Republican), nor for the maverick left-wing magazine, *Ramparts*, but for the radical and socialist *People's World*—a death wish? It was still another attempt to rewrite the Spanish war according to the insights of Paco *el Puto* (that's what we used to call him, anyhow). Its author was no common or garden variety of fascist, but a character who modestly described himself as "the man who lit the fuse to the Spanish Civil War" by chartering a plane for Paco to fly from the Canary Islands to North Africa to head the uprising of the generals who had sworn allegiance to the Republic.

I remembered the sermon I had preached from the pulpit of the First Unitarian Church of Los Angeles a few days earlier. Among other nasty things I had said:

> You know that since 1951 we have maintained Francisco Franco and his cohorts—with billions of dollars, with arms to suppress his people, with bases and airports and political muscle, taking over from his previous quartermasters Hitler and Mussolini, just as we took over from the defeated French in Vietnam—but with a difference.
>
> You know that our support . . . *alone* accounts for the continued existence of this 28-year-old fascist dictatorship. . . . In May

the universities of Madrid and Barcelona were closed by the government, with armed police occupying both campuses—but not before the students had made it plain what they felt: they ripped down photographs of Franco on the classroom walls, just as on April 28 they had held anti-Vietnam war demonstrations, burned the American flag and an effigy of Lyndon Baines Johnson. . . .

". . . there *is* a limit to American wealth," I had optimistically insisted, "poured down the rat-holes inhabited by such eager and greedy rats as Franco, Salazar, Chiang Kai-shek and Generals Ky and Thieu. There *is* a limit to American military power despite the Pentagon's obsession that if it only drops more bombs than have ever been dropped in the history of the world, the National Liberation Front and the people of Vietnam themselves will simply disappear.

Surely it is as traumatic to a loyal American to find himself rejoicing over the inevitable defeat of American arms in Vietnam, as it is to think of his beloved country as the object of fear, hatred and contempt throughout the world. But that is what is happening to us today and the ultimate freedom of the Vietnamese people is therefore guaranteed as fully as the freedom of the Spanish people. . . .

I remembered that a man had asked me for a copy of that speech and I had given it to him. He was from a newspaper called *España Libre* and I thought: Surely everything published in the U.S.A. about Spain—especially what is written in an antifascist paper—is clipped and mailed to Madrid.

I remembered that another man had approached me in the patio of the church after that speech and I had not recognized him for a moment, for after all, I had not seen him in many, many years and now he was . . . yes, he must be eighty.

He approached, a frail old man with a smiling face—and the eyes I immediately recognized—and he said, "I was not feeling very well today but I knew I had to come."

He clasped my hand in both of his and kissed me on the cheek and said, "I liked what you said about Aaron."

How could I tell Aaron's father that I was going to the land where his son had been sleeping for 29 years? And for such a purpose?

I suddenly recalled the contempt I had felt for Ernest Hemingway when I read a series of articles he wrote for *Life* in 1960 about his first visit to Spain after the war had ended. I fished the articles out of my files and reread the first and felt the same contempt:

It was strange going back to Spain again. I had never expected to be allowed to return to the country that I loved more than any other except my own and I would not return so long as any of my friends there were in jail. But in the spring of 1953 in Cuba I talked *with good friends who had fought on opposing sides* in the Spanish Civil War . . . and they agreed that I might *honorably* return to Spain if I did not recant anything that I had written and *kept my mouth shut on politics.* . . . (*Italics mine.–A.B.*)

Phrases I had underlined in red (naturally) leaped to my eyes: mock-heroic phrases like "if we were still at large"; contemptible phrases like "nothing could happen to Mary since she had never been in Spain in her life and knew only the very finest people. . . ." and, how at Biarritz "several of the very finest people were poised waiting to join us" and one of them had "a letter from Duke Miguel Primo de Rivera, then Spanish Ambassador in London."

Then he worked up a great dramatic production about crossing the frontier and when asked if he was Ernest Hemingway, "I pulled myself up to modified attention and said, '*A sus ordenes*' which means in Spanish not only at your orders but also at your disposal. I had seen it said and heard it said under many different circumstances and I hope I said it properly and in the right tone of voice."

Then, every time his party was stopped at checkpoints,

"I expected us to be detained or sent back to the frontier," but an Italian friend traveling with him "was an ex-cavalry officer who fought with Rommel and was a close and dear friend who had lived with us in Cuba. . . ."

Well, Hemingway had had a good excuse to return to Spain in 1959: LIFE had asked him "to write an account of the historic rivalry between the two great matadors of Spain, Luis Miguel Dominguin and Antonio Ordonez," and Hemingway had wanted to see the bullfights. Did I have as good an excuse? Would such a return be "honorable"? Certainly I had *no* friends who were among the very finest people, no good friends who had fought on both sides, no close and dear friends who had lived with me and had fought in Hitler's *Afrika Korps*, and if I ever got there I had no intention whatsoever of keeping my mouth shut on politics if there were any occasion to open it.

It suddenly occurred to me (*so* unreconstructed was my mind) that the man I had met in San Francisco three years earlier was either (1) insane, (2) irresponsible or (3) the cleverest fascist agent of them all.

I knew my books (and why not some of my articles and speeches?) had reached Madrid for I had seen them indexed in Spanish fascist literature written since 1939 to promote their interpretation of the great Crusade against the antichrist that had been led by The Most General.

That meant that they had taken this means to bring me to Spain for execution. I laughingly told this to my wife and she looked at me as though *I* were insane. I even said, "What the hell, when I went to Spain in 1938 I was prepared to die and if I'm going to die in Spain after 29 years I can't imagine a more fitting end."

I spoke of my theory to close and dear friends who have more political sense than I will ever have if I live to be twice my present age, and they said, "Absurd. If they wanted to knock you off there are lots of cheaper ways to do it than to pay your way to Barcelona.''

Being close and dear friends, they did *not* say what they should have said: "Who the hell do you think *you* are, anyhow?'' But these very same friends, after discounting the possibility of any harm coming to either of us, urged me to advise the American Civil Liberties Union of where I was going and what I was going to do; advise a local attorney, too, they told me; advise your literary agent in New York and advise the executive secretary of The Veterans of the Abraham Lincoln Brigade.

I did not advise the A.C.L.U.

II

Todo va mejor con Coca-Cola . . .

1

From the window of the *Caravelle* there was nothing to be seen of France. From Paris (where we had missed the *Iberia* flight the night before) to Barcelona takes no longer than an hour and a half and all we could see was the top of the cloud cover. I missed the days of the good old DC-3, when you could at least see something of the country unless you were on instruments all the way. From the jets, most of the time you see nothing.

Then, one hour after takeoff the clouds opened as though on cue and there were the Pyrenees, not exactly as I had seen them last from the train that left Ripoll on December 2, 1938, with bands playing, flags flying and the engine decked out in banners, flags and laurels—homage to the departing veterans. We arrived in Puigcerda and one hour after we had left it, the fascist planes bombarded it, a different form of *despedida*, to be sure, but one to which we had grown accustomed.

Looking down from the plane I thought I could detect the smugglers' trails over which we had climbed that January night so long ago. Maybe I did detect them after all, for we crossed the frontier and passed over Figueras and the fortress of San Fernando where we had been quartered for a week after our arrival. The Mediterranean was to our left, not so blue as I remembered it (it was November, after all) and something dreadful was going on inside me for I started to sob and could not control myself until my wife grasped my hand and pressed it. I said, "I'm sorry. I can't help it."

From Gerona on we were letting down and the coastline was drawing closer, and then we could see Barcelona and she

33

said, "Does it look much different?" and I said, "I never saw it from the air."

Certainly it looked larger and there were huge and hideous building developments to the south of the city, blocks of square apartment or factory buildings; it was hard to tell what they were.

The little man was standing behind the low barrier; the sun was shining and it was fairly warm. He smiled and waved and he seemed even smaller than he had three years before, although his mustache was much bushier. Then he disappeared and we were herded through a door toward a pair of booths marked POLICIA and I thought, frantically, Isn't he going to get us out of this or is he going to let the police grab me? I remembered Ernest Hemingway and was somewhat ashamed of my contempt for him, for the identical thing was happening to me, except that I had no occasion to say, "*A sus ordenes*," and probably would not have said it, if I had.

The cop in the booth looked long and hard at my passport (my wife had preceded me) and, just as Hemingway had described it, he did not look at me at all but, after a dramatic pause, stamped the passport and handed it back.

"This is Jaime Camino," I said to my wife in my worst Spanish, and, to him, "*Quiero presentar mi esposa, Sylviane.*"

What happened after that I cannot recall in any consecutive detail. Time collapsed like an accordion; we had arrived just after noon and suddenly it was night. I do not remember whether we came into town in a taxi or whether Jaime drove us. I do remember seeing a sign reading, *Bienvenida a Barcelona, Ciudad de Ferías y Congresos*. (What fairs? What congresses?) I remember a broad avenue and a huge, square and hideous building with a great sign reading: SEARS.

I remember seeing the symbol of the *Falange*, the yoke and arrows, erected in metal or wood, painted, beside the highway leading into the city, and felt the wound in my heart

"This is Jaime Camino," I said . . ."

opening again as it always does when I see that symbol (or the swastika).

There were enormous new buildings of glass and steel, of no particular grace or charm, but "modern," like similar buildings you will see in New York or San Francisco, Casablanca and Rabat, Paris or even East Berlin. They did not belong in Spain; for that matter, I doubt that they belong anywhere.

There were signs on almost every street and prominently displayed in every square, assuring us that *Todo va mejor con Coca-Cola*. I remembered there had once been a minor revolt against what the French were the first to call the "*Coca-colonization*" of Europe, but the rebellion must have petered out for *Coca-Cola* is supreme in all the capitalist countries of Europe, and even in North Africa. (Joan Crawford's *Pepsi-Cola* had not yet made its mark.)

Jaime took us to a hotel off a boulevard that looked familiar and I said, "Isn't this the Diagonal?" He smiled and said, "Yes. But now it is the Avenida del Generalisimo Francisco Franco."

At the modern hotel, modest but quite well-appointed, a dark young man at the desk who could have been a typecast Hollywood Spanish pimp with long sideburns, insisted on speaking very acceptable English when addressed in Spanish (good or bad). He said, "Passports," and when we both presented them he pushed my wife's back across the desk smiling, saying, "I do not need the woman's passport."

I looked at him with anger and at my wife, puzzled, and she said, "We're in Spain, darling—remember?"

Jaime said something about our getting a discount at the hotel because the manager was his friend and suddenly he was gone, promising to return in time to take us out to dinner.

He did. We walked and apparently I talked in bad French and worse Spanish, asking questions he never got a chance to answer because I had asked another.

We walked on the Avenida and came to the Paseo de Gracia and turned right and suddenly I was back in 1938, one of the two times I had been given a 48-hour pass, except that the *plátano* trees were bare now and the cars madly careening down the street had their lights on, instead of being blind. There *were* open trenches in the streets but they were not the result of bombing. They were for new construction on the subways. You could smell the sewers.

We ate at a restaurant that wasn't there in 1938, which was called *La Puñalada*, which Jaime said meant a stab—at least, he made the gesture when I asked the meaning of the word. From that time until we left there is nothing but a rising and swirling memory of sights, sounds and smells and tastes, of a mediocre wine and very good food (*comida típica de Cataluña*), which my wife informed me later, to my horror, consisted of many things I simply will *not* eat: clams and mussels, squid!—and which I ate with relish when I was not talking, asking, remembering how little there had been to eat those times before and how badly what little there was had been prepared.

Then we were on the Paseo again and walking and I was seeing buildings I remembered and asked, "Where's that melting house?" (in French, because I could not remember the word for melting in Spanish, although it is practically the same), but Jaime and his collaborator, Román Gubern, who had joined us in the restaurant, both knew immediately what I meant and said, "Gaudí's house? It's right down there." There it was: the incredible construction by Catalonia's greatest architect, a huge building without a single straight line to be found, inside or out.

I asked them if they knew the story I had been told about it—that Antonio Gaudí, building it on the commission of a very rich woman and her husband, so that it *would* not have a single straight line, finally became angered when it was finished; and the owners, pointing at the curving music room, demanded to know what sort of musical instrument they could put in it. Gaudí said, "Well, you could take a violin and hang it from the ceiling by a string." Neither of them had ever heard the story and it probably never happened anyhow. Now, they told me, the house was occupied by offices, huge luxury apartments and a few smaller ones—the crazy house.

"Then," I said, "we must be near the Majestic," and they said, "A couple of blocks." I had never stayed at the Majestic during my two trips to Barcelona, but Vincent

Sheean had lived there and Herbert Matthews and Robert
Capa and Luis Quintanilla, the artist; and Edwin Rolfe, the
poet-soldier of the Lincoln Battalion, had kindly allowed me
to take three baths in one day in his small apartment on my
first trip from the front, and to his amazement, there was
boiling water every time.

The Majestic did not look like the Majestic at all. Except
for its façade it had been rebuilt inside. The great dining room
that, once I had moved to San Francisco, always reminded me
of the Garden Court of the Palace Hotel (or *vice versa*) was
gone with its overhead glass dome under which Rolfe and Joe
Taylor and I and a couple other soldiers on leave had sat one
night when the city was being bombed, and watched the
searchlights through the glass and waited for it to fall onto our
heads. In its place, two or three other dining rooms, large and
small, had been built, and strangely enough this was a major
disappointment. So were the luxury items on display in glass
cases in the lobby, jewels and purses, *Agua Lavanda Puig* and
Chanel #5 and all the rest.

But the Plaza de Cataluña with its great fountains was the
same (except that the fountains were not running during the
war); the statues were still there, some hideous, some lovely,
and suddenly where there was a bank that night, I saw the
building as it had been in 1938, with a huge red banner hanging from roof to sidewalk with great white letters proclaiming
a slogan that would not return to mind, and suddenly Jaime,
seeing me looking at that corner said, "I'm told that during the
war that was the headquarters of the Communist Party of
Catalonia."

"Where *were* you during the war?" I asked, forgetting
his age for the moment, as I had forgotten everything else I
knew except the sense impressions of 29 years earlier. He
smiled and said, "I was born three months after the

Generalisimo's uprising," and certainly that was an astonishing fact to contemplate.

We were walking and we were walking and the weather was mild and the contradictions began to appear: not only the *Coca-Cola* signs or the plaques on buildings indicating that American companies were everywhere, but in the bookstores, in addition to what you would expect to find—Spanish editions of every inconsequential best seller in the United States—there were prominently displayed new editions of the works of Marx and Engels and when I turned a bewildered face to Román Gubern he smiled and said, "These are classics of social literature," which did not seem to be an adequate explanation for their presence in that time and place.

"Can you buy *For Whom the Bell Tolls?*" I asked (ah, Hemingway, forgive me my contempt).

"Not openly," I was told, "but it can be found."

"*Los Antinorteamericanos?*" I asked Jaime and he shook his head, but Román said, "I met a man who read it—he found it in the Burgos prison."

"How? *What!*" I stutterred and he shrugged.

This small piece of information was almost as dizzying as the Ramblas themselves, which I had remembered as much narrower and with small sidewalk tables (but, of course, it was winter) and the wooden flower stands were now permanent structures, closed at night by sheets of glass and metal netting. But the Ramblas were still the Ramblas and the whores were there, strolling as they had strolled, and when I commented on them Jaime said, decorously, "There are probably more public women in Barcelona than in any other city in the world—"

"Except Saigon," I said, "no?"

"*Supongo*," he said.

I was only looking at the girls, the honky-tonk bars, the drunken American sailors, the novelty shops that sold every-

thing from the classic leather *botas* to the endless cheap reproductions in wood and metal of Don Quixote and Sancho
Panza, imitation medieval swords and battle-axes in natural
sizes and in miniature, but my wife said, "Are you looking for
bomb damage from the war?"

Most of it had been down near the port, for the fascists
were very careful not to bomb the rich, residential *barrios*
abandoned by their friends who were in the "Nationalist" zone
or sitting out the war on the *Côte d'Azur* in France.

"No," I said, "but look," and pointed to the walls of
buildings where there were still shrapnel scars and bullet holes
to be plainly seen.

We stopped in a bar on the Plaza Real and had a cognac,
which was better than the cognac we had had during the war,
which all the American volunteers called paint remover. We
ate again—*comida típica*—the white sausages and white beans
that are called *butifarra con judías blancas* and neither of our
hosts could explain why the beans were called white Jewesses.

So great is the power of the juices secreted by the adrenal
glands, that it was possible for us to walk all the way back to
the hotel despite the 10-hour nonstop flight from Los Angeles
to Paris, the sleepless night in the Air Hotel at Orly, the flight
to Barcelona and the additional 14 hours we had been awake
since our arrival.

Street corners and individual buildings leaped at me, crying to be recognized again, and I could not understand how a
total of 96 hours in a city, some 29 years before, could have
made so profound an impression on my mind.

I recalled the second time I was there, that time with Joe
Hecht, who survived two years in Spain to be killed heroically
in his first action in Germany in 1945. We had hunted a public
bathhouse on the Rambla de las Flores and we found one. We
had climbed into individual tubs of steaming water and then,
remembering, we shouted for the attendant, yelling, "*Jabón!*

Jabón! No hay jabón!" and the attendant finally arrived and shrugged and said, "*Camaradas*, there *is* no soap," and that had been one of the major frustrations of 1938.

I remembered Aaron, who had gone on leave to Barcelona just before we crossed the Ebro—Joe Hecht had given him a couple condoms—and when I chided him, saying he would not patronize a whore (because I could not do such a thing myself), he had said, "Of course I will. This may be the last chance in my life to sleep with a woman." And it was. (And where, I thought, is Santa Coloma de las Planes?)

On one corner of the Paseo de Gracia I stopped and remembered: There had been a bookstore there and there had been a young woman in charge and she had had the most magnificent breasts I had ever seen (no bra). On the tip of her left breast, just over the nipple, she had pinned to her skintight sweater a tiny silver pin—a hammer and sickle. In a rather pathetic attempt to strike up an acquaintance, I had given her an American cigarette which she carefully put away in a cheap metal case "for later," as she said, and turned to wait on another customer.

I wondered where she was now, if she had survived some other frustrated lover who had later denounced her for that silver pin, and I thought, good God! she would be at least 49 years old, more likely 54 and in no more mood for horseplay than she was when the unshaved foreigner in a torn and dirty uniform had offered her a butt in hopeful exchange for something Aaron was willing to pay for with the coin of the realm.

We did not get to bed till after one o'clock, and it seemed to me that it was careless of the hotel not to have placed crisscross paper strips across the windowpanes, as they had been on the windows of the Hotel Gran Via off the Plaza de Cataluña the time I stayed there with Joe Hecht in November 1938. Now it was November 1967 and as I fell asleep I expected an air-raid siren to blow any minute but nothing happened until the waiter arrived the next morning at 11 with our breakfast on a tray.

2

The basic coin of the realm is still the *peseta* but it no longer bears the shield of the Republic. Every coin down to a ten *centimo* piece shows a profiled portrait of The Most General and it says, believe it or not, *Francisco Franco, Caudillo de España por la Gracia de Dios*.

Of course, when they speak of it at all, the Spanish wits have changed it to *por la Desgracia de Dios*, which does not mean disgrace so much as it means misfortune, mishap or affliction (which is a better joke). They have also changed the slogan to "Everything goes worse (*peor*) with *Coca-Cola*" or "Everything goes better without (*sin*) *Coca-Cola*," but they drink it all the same, just as they have been swallowing The Leader for the last 38 years and will continue to stomach him until they vomit—or he finally dies.

But we had not heard the anti-Franco or the anti-*Coca-Cola* jokes at that point and we spent the next day reading the screenplay Jaime had given us, which had the English title, *Spain Again*.

It was something of a disappointment, although we had been prepared—realizing some of the problems faced by film-makers and other artists under such a regime—for a story that would say nothing worthy of our time or effort. I had been prepared before I came to say, "I'm very sorry for the money you (or whoever) spent to bring me here, but I cannot work on such a thing as this."

It was a disappointment because it said so little, being largely devoted to the romance between the returned American doctor, David Foster, and the young María who was the daughter of his nurse and sweetheart of the Spanish war.

I could not believe in this romance for a moment. After all, the man was in his early fifties, the young woman in her early twenties and she immediately learns that he is married (his wife stays too conveniently in Mallorca during the medical congress), that he is remaining in her country no more than ten days, that he had been her mother's lover before she was born.

Then the thing began to hit me. First—creative imagination, no doubt—was the emotion displayed by the American doctor as his plane lets down to land at Barcelona and the other American doctor traveling with him (he is a Texan) says:

THOMPSON: . . . (Looking out the window over David's shoulder) Man—it's a beautiful city. And mighty large. Has it changed much?

DAVID: I suppose. . . . I never saw it from the air.

If Camino's first feature film could have been called revolutionary because it admitted that Spanish women sometimes commit adultery, this one simply could not be made.

Here was a film, written by a Spaniard (two of them) in Franco's black Spain, whose protagonist was an American who had fought on the "wrong" side of the war that Franco "won." Yet he did not wear horns. He was not an agent of Moscow nor an international Communist assassin—which is what Franco's propaganda said we were. He was an extremely kind and *simpático* man for whom the audience was expected to "pitch" (as they say in Hollywood) and with whom the audience would most certainly identify in every way.

How do you explain a thing like that? Jaime had said the first version of the script—the one we were reading—had been approved by the censorship. How could that be? He said they had some objections (I'll bet!) they had not yet reduced to writing. He had told me that all films made by Spanish companies were subsidized by the appropriate ministry up to 60 percent of the production cost—*if* they were approved.

But this approval had not gone that far; it was a tentative approval. The money would not be forthcoming until the final script was read and the film itself had been screened for the appropriate authorities. (Could they have smelled a rat?)

Even so, I was hard put to understand how such a story could even have won tentative approval unless it was a reflection of the widely announced "liberalization" the regime had proclaimed the year before. I thought about that. A couple paragraphs from the speech I had made in Los Angeles a week earlier echoed in my head:

. . . Franco's cabinet is split—and scared stiff. Why? Because Spain desperately wants to enter the Common Market. Hence, the alleged "liberalization" of the regime, announced last year. But the liberalization was taken literally and now thousands demonstrate regularly, shouting, "Liberty! Liberty! No trials! Democracy, yes! Dictatorship, no!" and even "Franco, no!"

A charming example of this liberalization was noted by the Associated Press and United Press on Wednesday of this week, reporting on the first elections held in Spain in 30 years. ". . . an estimated half of the nation's voters stayed home," said the report from Madrid. (That explained the election posters we had seen the night before, across every one of which some subversive character had scrawled—*No vota!*)

"Those who did vote—married persons and unmarried family heads and breadwinners—trooped to the polls to cast ballots for a parliamentary minority composed of candidates they knew would win anyway. About 16,000,000 were eligible to vote for 108 Congressmen. . . . These account for about 18 percent of the 563 seats of the Cortes. All other members have been elected already. They belong to professional associations, the National Movement—the only permitted political organization—the National Council and the 25 allotted for personal selection by Francisco Franco. . . ."

In April of 1967 student demonstrations had continued for several days and the government had answered—by promulgating a decree drafting students into the army who were found "guilty of poor conduct or poor citizenship." The identical thing had happened in Vietnam the first weeks in October of that year, scarcely surprising in a country whose *Caudillo* (*Duce*, *Führer*), General Ky, if not appointed by the Grace of God, at least had said he had only one hero—Adolph Hitler. So much for liberalization, but—there was the script.

Before we got a chance to discuss it Jaime appeared with his girlfriend, Martha (Martita), who, he said, was 30 years old and looked at least eighteen. She was a "cutie-pie" from Argentina and she was an excellent professional photographer. I could not understand a single word she said for at least two weeks because she not only inflected her Spanish in another way, but she habitually spoke without moving her lips and with machine-gun velocity.

That second night they took us—with Román—to another typical Catalan restaurant off the Ramblas in the Gothic *barrio* of the city. It is called *Los Caracoles* and was run by an enormously fat man named Bofarull—not *butifarra*—who was so much a part of the ambiance that he occasionally honored guests by signing their menus. And here there appeared the first omen, if you believe in omens (which I do not): at a promimently placed table near the entrance sat none other than Robert Taylor.

The last time I had seen this Man of Distinction in the flesh, he created a panic at the investigation of the motion-picture industry in October 1947 by the House Committee on Un-American Activities.

An elderly lady had fallen off a radiator in the corridor, trying to get a glimpse of the handsome fellow who stood before the Committee as a "friendly" witness and solemnly told it that if he had *ever* given the impression (and he had) that he was forced to play a role in a film called *Song of Russia*, it simply was not true because "nobody can force you to make any picture."

However, he did allow that ". . . it seems at the time there were many pictures being made to more or less strengthen the feeling of the American people toward Russia," and he certainly did strenuously object to appearing in it because "to my way of thinking at least" it did "contain Communist propaganda."

Ayn Rand, the later-to-be-rich reactionary novelist, had defined the nature of that Communist propaganda two days before Mr. Taylor made his sensational appearance. Speaking of *Song of Russia*, she had said, "There is a park where you see happy little children in white blouses running around. . . ." She said she had certainly never seen such children around the time she escaped from the Soviets (1926) and when asked, "Doesn't anybody smile in Russia anymore?" she replied, "Well . . . pretty much no."

Now, 20 years after he appeared before the Committee, Mr. Taylor did not look as though he could create such havoc that a 65-year old lady would fall off a radiator and bang her head. He looked distinctly aged, definitely debauched. I tormented my poor wife all through the *comida típica* by telling her that when we left I was going to march right up to Mr. Taylor's table and say, "You know, you don't look so hot these days."*

I was saved from making such a *gaffe*, certainly not by all the superior Catalan wine we drank that night, but by my belated recognition of the fact that I didn't look so hot myself and—more importantly—because Mr. Taylor and his entourage had left by the time we finished eating. There was nothing at his table to recall his refulgent personality except a large

---

* It was not long after this encounter that Taylor died—of cancer—and I suffered a belated *crise de conscience*.

place card reading: *Mr. Robert Taylor—In Person.*

There were more important things to worry about, however, than the parallel deterioration of friendly and unfriendly witnesses. There was the script, and the story conferences with Jaime and his collaborator began the following day.

3

In his pleasant apartment on Calle Balmes I discovered—by examining a framed diploma on the wall —that he rejoiced in the full name of Jaime Camino Vega de la Iglesia, and that he was a professor of piano! When I expressed interest in this fact, he told me that he was also an attorney but he no longer practiced the law, nor even the piano very much.

Our conferences sometimes began at noon; more often at five in the afternoon, after the midday meal (at three); sometimes at eleven or twelve at night, after dinner which had started at ten. (The Spaniards are insane that way.)

Most of the day the young director was otherwise occupied interviewing actors for his film. He held a long-distance conversation with Anthony Quinn, who was making a film on Mallorca and regretted that he could not star in *Spain Again* because he was signed up for the next five years. His salary, in any event, must have been at least twice the budget of the film (which was only $150,000).

Jaime was also scouting locations in Barcelona itself, for a tavern at which Doctor Foster used to eat when he came in from the front, for an old-man's home that would be inhabited by the man who used to run the tavern, for a *tablao* where the flamenco dancing would take place.

His girl friend Martita was scouting clothes from 1938,

an automobile of the period, a railroad car that could serve as a hospital train and would match the documentary footage Jaime had examined in Madrid before we came. He had a shooting date two weeks ahead, he had not found an American star and he was worried.

I was worried too, and told him so. I told him I did not believe in the romance and he ultimately agreed that the pair should not wind up in bed, as he had originally planned it. We agreed—after considerable discussion in three languages —that we should bring them, step by step, toward closer and closer mutual involvement, but we should not permit them to consummate their love—if only because the audience expected that they would, if not for better reasons.

What worried me more, I said, was the fact that the American protagonist simply did not *act*. He sat and people talked to him. He listened and he nodded and he smiled; he did not *do*.

"That's why you're here," he said to me. "To write him."

"Are you trying to say *you* couldn't write him? You even wrote lines for him that *I* spoke, 10,000 feet over Barcelona!"

"Coincidence," he said. "Oh, I could write him. But you can write him better." He smiled. "You're free to write anything you please, and I may shoot it—or maybe I won't."

"Just like in Hollywood."

"More Hollywood," he said, and flashed his dimples. "The way this picture started is like this: two gentlemen of Madrid, importers-exporters, decided to start a moving-picture company—*Pandora*."

"Do they know the legend?"

"I don't know. Anyhow, they had seen my first two pictures. They sent me a script and I read it. I sent it back, saying, if I never made another film I would not make that script. It was no good. Then they called me up and said, '*You* make a picture. Make *any* picture that you like.' There was only one condition—"

"One of them has a girl friend—"

"*Eso es*. Román and I started to write a very different story, but gradually it evolved into what we have today."

"And the girl friend has never appeared on screen?"

"Never."

"What does she do? I mean—"

"She's a dancer. She's one of the three best flamenco dancers in Spain today."

"*Eso es*."

"This weekend," Jaime said, "we're going to look at some locations. Would you and Sylviane care to come along?"

"Of course. Where are we going?"

"Well, you have read the script. We're going to see the Roman arch that Doctor Foster remembers from his previous visit. We're going to find a *masía*—you know, the farm where the pig is killed—"

"I don't like that scene, either," I said. "It doesn't seem to move the story along."

"It's symbolical," said Jaime. "Then we're going to look at the *manicomio*—the mental institution he visits, the destroyed town, and I must also find a church in a provincial town, a typical poor man's church."

"Where are these places? You have no place-names in the script."

"We will go," said Jaime casually, "to Tarragona, Reus, Falset; then we'll cross the Ebro at Mora la Nueva, through Mora de Ebro to Corbera and Gandesa in the Sierra Pandols."

I was silent. Rather, I was speechless. He had named some of the key places where we had fought and so many of us had agonized—so many died. Is this a dream or a nightmare? How could this *be*? I wondered. I looked at him.

The face across the desk from me was quite impassive, the melting bedroom eyes more veiled than ever.

4

The original plan was to start early in the morning, returning to Tarragona on the coast to sleep, and then come back to Barcelona. But plans have a way of being changed —especially in Spain—so we did not get started till late in the afternoon.

There were six of us jammed into the ancient *Mercedes*, which was filthy and had not been cleaned or washed in many months, and belonged to the young man who was driving it.

He was a German-Swiss named Martin Huber, whose hair hung to the nape of his neck. He spoke English with a combination German-British accent, German with a Swiss accent, French with a Spanish accent and Spanish with a French accent. He had been an actor of small parts in various countries in Europe and was now attached to Camino's film in some anomalous capacity. For some reason he was called Pipo—and I called him Pipo *el Tipo*.

On that trip everyone except my wife and I acquired a different name. Jaime became Jaime *Primero el Conquistador*. His chief of production was also named Jaime—Jaime Fernández Cid—and therefore he was Jaime *el Cid*. Martita became *Chiquita* or *Chiquita Banana*—and Camino promptly started to sing the song in a surprisingly well-trained baritone.

It was dark long before we approached Tarragona and therefore when we reached the triumphal arch of Bara that spans the ancient Roman road, and, a little further on, the monument reputed to be the tomb of Gnaius and Publius Cornelius Scipio (but probably is not), we had to examine them both with flashlights.

The Scipios captured the ancient town of Tarraco, which was the capital of an Iberian tribe called the Cessatani, in 218 B.C. The city itself, abounding in Roman ruins, has since been in the hands of the Carthaginians (who killed the brothers in 212 B.C.). Various notables such as Augustus and Hadrian had occupied it, not to mention the Visigoths who took it in 467 A.D. and were expelled in 711 by the Moors (they sacked and burned it), who held it for almost 400 years until the Spanish drove them out. The British and French have also occupied the place, but I was more impressed by the Roman aspects of the city, the only time I saw it in 1938 was before we crossed the Ebro, when some of us had 24-hour passes as a reward for high scores in a rifle contest.

For a fellow who was born in Harlem when, as my mother used to say, "it was a respectable neighborhood," I have always been queer for the Romans and cannot see anything they have left without becoming slightly dizzy.

This must be true of Camino, too, for his Doctor Foster, on the sentimental journey he takes with the young María, thinks:

DAVID'S VOICE (off): The Roman arch . . . the Romans survive, no matter what happens. Why didn't I pay more attention to them? . . . Romans, Carthaginians, Phoenicians, Egyptians, Trojans . . . all that remains of them are a few names and some stones . . . but the stones endure. . . .

The Romans had planned to endure, too; they felt they had a "commitment" to the far-flung populations they terrorized, colonized and benefitted with their public works projects, but you cannot see anything they left behind without taking your proper place in history—and remembering Shelley's "Ozymandias."

*

We reached Tarragona near midnight and checked into a hotel on a street I had walked before. (It used to be named after St. John. Now it is also named after The Most General. *Sic transit*.)

We went out to eat at a small bar a few doors away and I recalled that the last time I had strolled on that street, which leads down to the cliff overlooking the beach, there had been signs in all the windows—crudely lettered signs reading: *No hay tabaco* or *No hay comida*. One imaginative (and possibly provocative) fellow had even posted a sign reading, *No hay nada*.

There had been very little of anything in 1938, to be sure. We had a meager meal at a magnificently named (if meager-looking) place on the beach called the *Gran Hotel Nacional*, but it seemed there was no dearth of prostitutes in the half-deserted town and the other men went looking for a house while I wandered lonely as a cloud, wondering why I could not do the same.

Later we swam in the Mediterranean, which was as blue as it is in all the postcards. It was lukewarm and you could wade out almost a quarter of a mile before the water reached your waist. There were only one or two other people on the beach; the *cabañas* were abandoned, their striped canvas faded, and we felt very strange sunbathing in the middle of a war.

Twenty-nine years later there was a full moon and Sylviane and I went for a walk along the promenade above the beach. I pointed out to her—far down toward the shore—the remains of the Roman theater and baths, but we were too tired to walk that far.

Instead, we walked up into the town where part of the original Roman walls were incorporated into retaining walls bordering the steep streets, and you could touch the enormous unhewn blocks of the lowest course, still rough to the hand more than 2,000 years after the Scipios had had them laid.

I remembered that somewhere in the town (I could not remember where) there was a tombstone built into such a wall—the *stele* of a Roman charioteer whose metrical epitaph complained that he would rather have died in the circus than of a fever. He died young but his voice may still be heard.

*

Reus had been a mass of rubble during the war, the night we returned to our base from Tarragona. The marquee of a bombed-out theater offered *Tiempos Modernos, con Carlos Chaplin*. We had had to detour around the center of the city then, but now it was all cleaned up and we did not stop. We were going to visit the mental institution outside the town that was to provide a sequence in the film.

All that the script called for were a few silent shots of Dr. David Foster talking with the staff; the staff listening respectfully to him, and a *montage* of faces of the patients. The young María had refused to visit the institution with her older friend, saying that insane people frightened her, and David had agreed that she should wait outside.

This was too convenient, for it was while she was sitting in the rented car, waiting for him, that she accidentally came across a photograph of 30 years before showing the owner of the tavern, Manuel, her mother and the American doctor, with his arm around her shoulder.

We argued once more as we approached the institution, and I insisted that the sequence made no sense unless it could be used to bring the two together; unless María entered the hospital with David, watched him as he examined and talked to the patients and the staff, noticed how warmly he related to the poor *locos*. A *montage* of mad faces might have been symbolic, as the killing of the pig at the *masía* might also have been a symbol of the cruelty beneath the apparently placid surface of Spanish life, but the sequence made no sense.

Said the director, as he and *el Cid* were admitted to the institution, "You may write some scenes if you like." I liked, but wondered what sort of scenes could be written for such a location.

Pipo *el Tipo*, *Chiquita Banana* and Sylviane and I remained outside the high grilled fence, in the sun that was not any too warm. We stood and talked and Martita said (perhaps echoing the script) that she didn't want to go inside, either; the *locos* frightened *her*.

We smoked and waited for Jaime and his *jefe de producción* to consult the director of the hospital, find out if he would give permission for us to visit, too. There were some *locos* visible, whom we insisted (as did Dr. Foster) should not be called crazy but ill and Martita said, "O.K." (in English), "*enfermos. Es igual.*"

The sick men were watching us through the fence. They were gathered in a group and they had farming tools and were very badly dressed, even for working men. This seemed odd, for we had been told this was a private institution and if you were a patient in a private *manicomio* in Spain, your relatives had money.

After almost three-quarters of an hour a custodian unlocked the gates and these men came out and made a beeline for our group—or rather, me.

Their faces worked passionately; they had strange tics and they all cried, "*Cigarillos!* . . . *tabaco!* . . . *cigaros!* . . ." That was when I made a mistake: I handed one of them my package, thinking he would distribute them, but the others rushed him, grabbing for the pack. He fought his way free and with some semblance of sanity struggled against the group to return the pack.

One of them was mumbling something that I could not understand, but they all calmed down the moment I started to pass out the cigarettes individually. They asked for a light and went happily off to a distant field, where they apparently worked in the vineyards without supervision.

Martita came back from where she had been hiding (behind the car), and I asked my wife if she had understood what that one man was mumbling.

"Yes," she said, and spoke in Spanish. "He said, 'The Reds are coming . . . the Reds are coming . . . they're coming to get me and they'll get you, too.' "

"*No!*" I said, and she said, "Yes."

Then Jaime the First appeared with the other Jaime and we were all admitted.

If you have never visited such an institution you are due for a surprise, for with the exception of the very few violent or totally regressed patients, the majority seem just as normal as their doctors, just as the majority of inmates in our federal prisons seem *far* "better adjusted" than their guards.

The director of the institution, who wore a white coat (why?), was pleasant enough, but he was a compulsive talker. He talked so much that it was impossible most of the time to get a word in edgewise or even ask a question.

He took us on a conducted tour: we visited the laundries where women were washing and banging clothes on boards. They looked up and smiled as we went through. We visited a barn-like structure that had a fairly well-equipped theater; we visited a ward in which only one obviously ancient woman was in bed. We visited the kitchen and the dining room; everything was remarkably clean if scarcely ultramodern. We inspected private rooms that were Spartan in appearance, like any cell in any prison.

The little doctor talked and talked and talked and Sylviane said, in an aside to me, "He's *dying* to appear in the film." He brought out for our inspection two patients whom we talked to separately in a reception room. There was a uniformed nurse with us who had unlocked each door as we approached it and locked it again behind us, but the majority of the attendants were nuns of the Sisters of Charity of St. Vincent de Paul, and in the private rooms there was a crucifix over every solitary cot.

The first patient was a young girl the doctor had told us was a hopeless schizophrenic. She was not bad-looking, was about twenty-three. She wore no makeup and had pleasant features and she was alert. She was totally relaxed as the doctor questioned her, as Jaime asked her questions, and as she replied. She was also obviously happy.

The only thing patently wrong with her was that her happy and relaxed conversation made no sense. She was an uneducated girl who announced calmly that she was an intellectual, which is not impossible, for that matter. But she confided to us that she knew more than other people knew; she understood more than most people; she saw and heard things other people did not see or hear. What they were she never said and no one pressed her, and she took her leave as graciously—and as happily—as she had appeared.

The second patient was something else again. She was in late middle-age, perhaps 55, but she looked 70. Her graying hair was closely cropped and the director had told us that, although she came of a well-to-do family, when she was committed she had been filthy, in rags and infested by lice.

She sat in a straight chair and at first refused to answer any questions. She was apparently so unselfconscious or withdrawn that she was not even aware that mucous was dripping from her nose.

The director asked her over and over again who she was. She did not answer. "Come now," he said, "you know who you are; why don't you tell us?"

"*Soy nada*," the woman finally said, firmly.

"That's not true," the doctor said gently. "You're a person, just like all of us. It's not true that you are nothing."

"*Soy nada!*" the woman said vehemently now. "*Soy una mujer!*" She spit it out this time, looking at the floor of the room. "*Para ti, soy NADA!*"

Considering the centuries during which women were practically chattels, I wondered if such a derangement was peculiarly Spanish: "I'm a woman. To you, I'm *nothing*." Surely, it was less likely to have been prevalent under the Republic than before or since. But momentary reflection convinced me that the malady is still epidemic.

But, I thought, there *are* peculiarly Spanish manias: one is certainly anti-Communism (especially in high places); the other is religious mania which created the scornful word *beata* (blessed) to describe those pitiful women who go to mass several times a day.

In Constancia de la Mora's autobiography, *In Place of Splendor* (Harcourt Brace, 1939), there is an astonishing passage in which she describes the violent struggle the women who were caring for orphan children during the first days of the war had had to put up, to get the little girls to take off their clothing to be bathed. Previously these orphans had been cared for by the nuns, but the nuns had abandoned them out of fear of "The Reds."

"I picked up a sweet, black-haired little girl with great black eyes for my first attempt. I unbuttoned Enriquetita's filthy black flannel pinafore, peeled off her thick black stockings and worn shoes. Then came the battle. As I tried to unfasten her dirt-encrusted chemise, she began to struggle wildly, shouting something I could not quite understand—she lisped. Finally I made it out.

" 'It's a sin against modesty!' she wept. Enriquetita was four years old!"

("There are more public women in Barcelona . . ." Jaime had said. . . .)

5

As we approached the Ebro my excitement mounted. We stopped for lunch in Falset, a town I had passed through many times on many individual trucks and in convoys of *camiones*. The food was passable but the local wine, grown and bottled in the area, was excellent (if tart) and we bought some extra bottles to take back to Barcelona.

Past Falset the road began to climb and wind, but it was better than it had been 29 years earlier and Pipo *el Tipo* was an excellent driver, even if he seemed as obsessed by the mania for speed as the Spanish *choferes* themselves had been—and are.

Past Falset a sign pointed to Marsa (to the left) and further on, another (also to the left) indicated the road to Darnos. Both names loomed large in memory for they were villages where we had spent many weeks in rest positions, training new recruits, reprovisioning the battalion. I was positive that if we had entered Darnos (Give us? Give us this day?) I could have led the way from the small town with its abandoned tiny movie house, across the road and through the vine fields to the very *barranca* where Aaron and I (and Pavlos Fortis, the Greek leader of the first platoon) had slept together in a cave in the sandy soil of the gulley. There was also a railroad spur line running through the *arroyo*, and a railroad tunnel inside of which a huge and ancient (1889) railway gun was mounted on a flatcar. Once a week they hauled it out at night, loaded it and fired—once.

It was all I could do to control my trembling body. I tried to ignore the inevitable *Falange* symbol (ten feet high) at the entrance to the towns, but each time I felt anginal pains that could not, I was sure, be ascribed to my infarction of 14 months earlier.

I wanted to ask Jaime to drive to Darnos and to Marsa, too, but I knew there was no time, so I was silent. Then, suddenly the river appeared and we entered the town of Mora la Nueva on whose asphalt sidewalk I had slept one night the first week in April of 1938, after we retreated across the river and the bridge was blown behind us.

Suddenly I could see and *feel* a blanket I had picked up the next night, when we moved back from the river to get away from the shells the fascist tanks were lobbing at us, and had moved into a former artillery emplacement up the hill. It was bitter cold and I stumbled across the blanket in the dark and overcome with joy I draped it across my shoulders. Then I felt that it was wet. It was wet and *sticky* and I struck a forbidden match and saw that it was soaked in coagulating blood, and cold as I was I threw it to the ground and sat hunched up under an olive tree the rest of the night.

The iron bridge that had been lying half in the muddy river the last time I saw it had been replaced by a graceful, reinforced concrete bridge and as we crossed it I said out loud, "We swam there one night—" pointing to the beach above the town of Mora de Ebro, across the river.

"Is this where you crossed in the offensive?" Sylviane asked, taking my hand as she had in the *Caravelle* crossing the Pyrenees, and I said, "No, further upstream, halfway to Flix."

Flix . . . a name. *Romans, Carthaginians, Phoenicians, Egyptians, Trojans . . . all that remains of them are a few names and some stones . . .* but these places are all *real*; they are all around me and I am here where I never expected to be again in my lifetime—Flix and García and Ascó, Fatarella where we found the Italian *intendencia* during the offensive when we were moving forward for a change, and there was not only chocolate in paper rolls, and warm beer and bad quality

Italian shoes, but sardines in tomato sauce. . . . We are near Villalba de los Arcos and Batea, names of agony and exaltation, meaningless to those who did not share with us—

From Mora la Nueva, Mora de Ebro looked exactly as I had seen it last during our final retreat from the Ebro sector when Negrín had spoken before the League of Nations and announced the withdrawal of the Republic's volunteers.

We were in Mora de Ebro now . . . it was precisely at *that* point we just passed where there was a truck, during the April retreats, and there was a little girl six years old sitting on the tail gate crying as we walked by toward the bridge, saying over and over, *"Mama perdida! Mama perdida!"* I wondered if she ever found her mother and if she did where did they live and was she married now, divorced or dead.

It was beyond Mora in the hills that a handful of us had sat all day in heat that almost drove you into the ground, watching for the fascist tanks that finally came—and then we crossed the river. It was April.

It was on this straight road leading *out* of Mora toward the front that I sat in the cab of a truck later that year, returning from Gratallops behind us on the other shore (there is a Cantallops, too) after stopping the mail (because Negrín had spoken). We were returning to Brigade headquarters in the Sierra Caballs and suddenly over our head there appeared two fighter planes in final combat.

One was ours and one was theirs and they were no more than 200 feet off the ground and theirs was on the tail of ours and he was climbing and diving, doing snap-rolls, his red wing-tips flashing, zooming, leveling off and then split-s-ing out of it but he was hit and he spun into the ground a half a mile away and we heard and felt the explosion and saw the flames and thick black smoke rising and we knew there was no need to stop and help.

*

Excerpts from a diary:

August 5, 1938– . . . Late at night–12:30 a.m. (Aug. 5)–we pulled out, marched through the outskirts of Corbera, down the Corbera-Gandesa road to a point about three miles from Gandesa, and relieved two battalions of the 11th, entrenched there. The men went into poor, shallow trenches, dug into vine fields 200-500 meters from the fascist lines; no communication trenches–flat terrain, impossible to get in and out without being observed and sniped at. . . .

August 7—Relieved last night at midnight by the 27th Division (and glad to get out of that sinister hole). Marched 15 kilometers down the Gandesa-Corbera road toward Mora de Ebro—passing through Corbera—a horrible shambles. . . . Smell of the dead rotten-sweet through the dead streets, the shell-like houses, the very trees torn to shreds—nothing is left of the town. . . .

The road runs straight as a ruler through the town and the few houses on the road itself are mostly warehouses, as they had been in 1938. There are one or two tiny shops but nothing else. There were no more than three or four people visible.

Pipo (that type) parked on the left side of the road for some reason or other and we had not moved more than ten feet from the car before two *Guardia Civil* appeared from nowhere and tagged him.

They still wear their absurd, winged, black patent-leather hats but they no longer evoke the image García Lorca created of them for all time, and for which, among other cogent reasons, the fascists in Granada murdered him on August 19, 1936:

CORBERA: "It was exactly as I had seen it on August 7, 1938 . . ."

> *Los caballos negros son,*
> *las herraduras son negras.*
> *Sobre las capas relucen*
> *manchas de tinta y de cera.*
> *Tienen, por eso no lloran,*
> *de plomo las calaveras. . . .*

Their black horses with black horseshoes are motorcycles with black tires now and they do not wear capes stained with ink and wax; but since their skulis are still made of lead, they do not weep.

These two had the mugs of typecast thugs and they made a great show out of the parking ticket, their pistols in their leather holsters far from *inconcretas*, as Lorca put it, their faces unblemished by any smile when it was explained by Jaime that the young man was a foreigner, did not know the traffic regulations, had left his international driver's license in his other clothes. No other car was in the town, nor passed through it so long as we were there.

The town, when seen from the road, had seemed the same as ever, but when the *Guardia Civil* roared off to other easy conquests and we rounded the building on the highway and started to climb into the town itself—there *was* no town.

It was exactly as I had seen it on August 7, 1938, except that no old-fashioned wedding portraits hung crooked on the exposed walls of humble apartments, no bedsprings or mattresses or children's toys or chamber pots lay in the great craters where the bombs had finally exploded; no torn sheets or bloody blankets could be seen; no kitchen utensils or broken crockery were scattered all around.

We climbed into the cobbled streets. Heavy wooden doors had been bolted over the entrances to empty shells. The blue whitewash of the inner walls had not quite faded out; the broken red tiles of the missing roofs lay in heaps everywhere, and while I knew it was absurd I *thought* that I could still detect the crushed and rotting dead.

There had been few enough of them—perhaps 50—for the town had been officially evacuated. But the old men, the old women and the children who died in Corbera between the fifth and seventh of August had not wanted to leave the only homes they knew; they came back, secretly, at night. Corbera was scarcely a military objective; it was not even a crossroads; there were no arms or munitions there. There was nothing around it but the same well-kept vineyards and olive fields that you will find today.

Jaime said something very fast and Sylviane translated: "If Gypsies who are living here come out, don't answer them and don't give any money."

We saw no Gypsies but there were some boys playing in the ruins and after an hour of scouting a good house for Dr. Foster to walk into and look out of its empty window, and a likely wall that could be pulled down easily to bring the frightened young María into his arms for the first time, we started down.

We tried to enter one of the empty houses by pushing on the heavy door and a voice cried out to us in Catalan, saying, "That's not your house! You can't go in it."

An aging woman had appeared in another doorway with a broom in her hand, and we were as startled as though the dead of 1938 had risen from the ruins. We spoke to her and she explained:

"Nobody lives there but nobody is supposed to go inside."

The house in which she obviously lived had three stories. The entrance, which we could see, was scrupulously clean. She said, Yes, she had lived there during the war. Yes, she had had two children—now grown up—who narrowly escaped the bombing. When I asked her why so small a town should

CORBERA: ". . . the same well-kept vineyards and olive fields . . ."

have been bombed—surely it had had no military importance—she looked at me and said, *"Pues,* there was a war. The front was near."

"Who bombed it?" I asked, playing the *provocateur,* "the Reds?" (That's what they call them in Spain today, at least in public.)

"No," she said, "the Nationalists."

"I'd love to see the inside of her house," my wife mumbled. I said, "Ask her."

Sylviane shook her head but a few minutes later I urged her to ask permission and she did and the woman nodded

SYLVIANE: "I'd love to see the inside of her house . . ."

graciously and said what I knew she must say: "My house is your house," and led the way.

The others stayed outside. There were three stories. There was nothing in the house that could possibly have been called furniture: a worn-out bureau and a sagging bed; a few hard chairs, a few old utensils. One or two small pictures on the walls. No crucifix, but a chromo of the Christ and little children.

The woman's children had grown up and gone away. Her son lived in Barcelona; he was a chemist. That is, he was a chemist in the day time; at night he was a taxi driver. You need two jobs, she said, to keep alive.

With enormous pride and dignity, the woman insisted on showing us every room on every floor, including the attic with the translucent sheets of cheap plastic that kept out some rain in the rainy season. In the attic she had stores of what I had previously seen kept on the ground floor in the dirt-floored country houses: drying apples hanging from the rafters, sacks of *avellanos* and dried figs, crocks of olive oil.

"No wine?" I said with a smile and she shook her head. "Downstairs," she said.

Suddenly she scooped up handfuls of hazelnuts and started to pour them into Sylviane's open purse. She reached down two strings of drying apples and handed them to me. She wanted to give us figs but we had nothing in which to carry them, and we thanked her and praised the house (as my mother used to say, "You could have eaten off the floor.") and started down.

In the basement she showed us her pride and joy—a present from her son in Barcelona: a relatively new and gleaming white electric washing machine. Her pleasure in this modern gadget did not seem diminished in the least by the fact that the house had no hot-water heater and the electricity, as she explained, was "not strong enough." It never had been used.

CORBERA: ". . . there was a small procession: a bridal party . . ."

Outside again, we shared the hazelnuts and apples and walked some more through the destroyed town. I remembered the fading plaque on a building on the highway: something to the effect that this place was under the protection of some governmental administration "for devastated areas." I wondered how they were "protecting" it and asked Jaime why it had never been rebuilt. He shrugged and said, *"No sé."* (Later I asked seven other people the same question. Their answer was the same: they did not know. One, cynically, ventured the opinion that Paco wanted it that way—Paco is the diminutive of Francisco—so that anyone who had any odd ideas could take a look at Corbera and see what happened.)

The huge and beautiful church was locked and bolted.

Through a crack in the enormous door you could see that it was gutted, though its walls were still intact. There was no roof. A house down the street had some fading letters painted on its door, reading, "Taken Over by the C.N.T." This was the Anarchist trade union during the Republic.

There was another church—and cemetery with cypress trees—in the distance that had not been there in 1938 and suddenly Martita noticed that in the street far below us there was a small procession: a bridal party with the bride in white, was walking along the highway from the distant church.

A Spanish novelist once published a book called *The Cypresses Believe in God*. With the exception of the *beatas*, I wondered who else did.

6

We got back to Barcelona late that night. In Gandesa, the same hole it had always been, we had found a "poor man's church." In a workingman's café the drinkers in their pathetic Sunday clothes looked at our two women with admiration and some scorn, for Sylviane was wearing a brilliant red coat with a fur collar and Martita was in her favorite mini-*culottes*.

Seeing that town again which we had tried so hard to take (after the April 1938 retreats it had become the main base for Mussolini's "volunteers"), it was hard to believe that it had figured prominently in our history—on two occasions.

Much of the brigade had been cut off and surrounded near Gandesa in late March of that year. That was where we lost our Chief of Staff, Robert Merriman, and his political officer, Dave Doran. That was where they had been so prodigal of their *matériel* that they actually sniped at us with artillery; that was where the Moors' cavalry attack (an anach-

ronism but just as terrifying as such attacks have always
been) had cut men down like sheaves of grain.

From Gandesa the survivors of the XVth International
Brigade had made their way through the enemy lines back to
the Ebro where many of them had swum in the ice-cold, swift
and muddy tide, for the first—and last—time.

Writing in the *New York Times* for April 5, 1938, Herbert L. Matthews said: "So all in all one can say about 150 out
of the original 450 can be accounted for today. Almost certainly more of them will turn up in the coming days, and some
may be prisoners. But lots of very fine men are not going to be
seen again."

During our offensive in July we had Gandesa almost
surrounded, but the automatic mountain artillery, the bombing
of our positions all around it in the Sierra Pandols, had pinned
us down—for good.

Today it is still a crummy provincial town with few men
old enough to remember the war or its key position in our
advance—and our retreat.

We came back through Mora again and to my surprise,
Pipo, in compliance with some swift remark Jaime had made,
suddenly turned off the highway that led onto the bridge, and
drove parallel to the river to the point overlooking the
wretched beach that I had pointed out.

We got out and looked at the river. It was flowing as
swiftly as ever, its waters roiled with mud; occasional broken
branches floated by, and whole, uprooted bushes. I stood looking down into it at the point where, one August night, after
many weeks of filth and exhaustion we came down by companies from the front to bathe and get fresh underwear and
outer clothing. I was halfway between tears and laughter,
looking at it and remembering that as I had crossed it for the
last time in September 1938, in a truck that rode bumpily over
the pontoon bridge that was parallel to the collapsed original, I
had thought of Aaron. . . .

THE EBRO: ". . . halfway between tears and laughter . . ."

*

The story conferences began again and the arguments—which were always amicable. I felt that the sequence at Corbera, as written, was no more important than the original sequence in the mental institution: it too was a silent montage of David Foster and the young María, wandering through the ruins of the little town on the hillside. They were secretly observed by a man with a hard, unshaven face (why?). One of the walls fell and María took shelter in David's arms.

"You may write a scene," Jaime said, and I said I would.

The story conferences were so irregular and Camino was so preoccupied with preproduction problems that we had our time pretty much to ourselves. It was therefore possible for us to take the second weekend off to visit Sylviane's relatives in Perpignan, and to walk for hours in the streets of Barcelona.

In addition to the patent contradiction of seeing works by

SPAIN AGAIN: ". . . and the young María, wandering through the ruins . . ."

Carlos Marx and Federico Engels openly for sale in the bookstores, we visited another contradiction—the Picasso Museum. This is housed in a magnificent palace on the Calle Moncada that dates from the Middle Ages, and since almost everything displayed was very early Picasso, almost all of which had been given by that notorious Communist to a personal friend whose name was inscribed on almost every piece of work, perhaps it is not so great a contradiction. (Incidentally, people we met felt it was a bad political mistake for Picasso—still living in the South of France—to refuse to visit Spain. "He would be treated like a hero," they said. They thought Pablo Casals, himself a Catalan, should also return, if only to upset the regime of The Most General, who would not dare do anything to harass either citizen of the world.)

We ate at the Majestic Hotel twice and while the food was good the atmosphere was unbearable. The hotel seemed to cater exclusively to tourists, all of whom were at least 70 years old—what very few there were. I could not connect our lunches there with the meals I had had during the war with Ed Rolfe and Sheean and Matthews. Much better food (and cheaper) may be found at the fish restaurant, *Casa Costa*, down at the port, and Sylviane was beginning to complain that the Spanish could cook nothing but fish and chicken, anyhow, and she is right.

We visited the cathedral in the *Barrio Gótico*, which had been started in the late 13th Century. We inspected Antonio Gaudí's masterpiece, the Expiatory Temple of the Holy Family, which has been in process of construction for more than 80 years and is nowhere near completion.

It seems that Gaudí changed his mind about design several times and died without leaving any completed plans. There has been a running debate ever since as to whether the *Sagrada Familia* should be finished or abandoned. One school of thought says, "It's from another era and the fortune it would cost to finish it could be used to better purposes." The opposition says that after all, it *is* a masterpiece of the human spirit and should therefore be completed. Both are right but the construction continues at a snail's pace and a committee of architects is in constant consultation, trying to figure out what the Catalan genius had in mind.

We took a taxi to the great church on top of Tibidabo. ("I will give to you," said the Lord, speaking in Latin unto St.

John Bosco in April 1886—and one month later a board of Catholic gentlemen gave him the peak of the mountain behind the city.) When we reached the top some workmen were struggling against rain, cold and wind to hang a gigantic Red Cross on the central tower, for the annual Red Cross campaign is celebrated for one week in Spain, probably with more zeal than the American United Crusade could mount over a month.

Tibidabo is also an expiatory temple and it was fascinating to learn that it is possible not only to expiate your own sins by ordering a mass, and not only the sins of your family, your company, your city and your country. It is also possible to "bring relief to all the deceased. Tibidabo has organized," says its publicity, "the EXPIATORY WORK IN FAVOUR OF THE DECEASED."

Montjuich (Catalan for Mountjew) was far more interesting, at least to me. My wife had abandoned the Catholic Church when she was scarcely nubile and no matter how magnificent the design or execution (*Notre-Dame*, the *Sainte-Chapelle*, *Saint Germain-des-Près*) I am invariably depressed by the votary candles for sale, by the little locked boxes next to every chapel begging offerings for "the sick poor," "missions to the heathen," "orphan children" and for every single saint (What do they *do* with them?). The final destruction of my wife's faith was completed, she had told me, by her first visit to Spain in 1953, when she was appalled by the "treasure" and the jewels worn by the Virgin and the other statues in the cathedral of Sevilla, while the poor and ragged *beatas* beat their heads upon the flagstone floor.

Montjuich is a fortress (and an amusement park, now) and the fortress is a military museum, which did not interest Sylviane at all. It is possible to be impressed, of course, by the ingenuity, design and craftsmanship of the endless implements of torture and death man has invented to use upon his fellowman, but that is all.

I was curious to see what place our little war occupied in the museum, but aside from photographs of the brilliant generals who finally took Barcelona without a struggle when the Catalan front collapsed in January 1939, and aside from a few captured arms (most of them, naturally, of Russian origin), there was no mention of the Great Crusade.

The Crusader himself was (temporarily) immortalized in the outer courtyard. There is an equestrian statue of Paco, somewhat slimmed for the purpose but still a fat little man on a fat big horse, his right arm extended in a gesture that might be called *Pax Fascista*, if there were such a thing. On the pedestal we were informed that the absurdity had been erected to express "the gratitude of the people of Barcelona," with the exception, no doubt, of that half a million men, women and children who climbed the Pyrenees in midwinter and dropped, exhausted, on the freezing roads to France, to escape their liberation.

Mountjew? How did the name of my people become attached to this small mountain? The simplest explanation lies in the fact that the ancient site yielded tombstones from long before the 10th Century, engraved in Hebrew letters, which the Spanish have placed on exhibition in the castle and faithfully translated for the heathen Catholics. (In the Barrio del Call, one such stone is embedded in a wall and reads: "The Holy Rabbi Samuel Hasareri did not end his life in the year 692. He resides with other remains of the time of the Jews in this house, built over the ruins of that founded by St. Dominick.")

For centuries the fortress was also a prison and the custodian on duty, who was intrigued by my wife's fluent Spanish, made a slip of the tongue when he told us it had been used for such a purpose until five years before.

"Prisoners?" my wife said with her best naive smile. "What sort of prisoners?"

"*Pues, politic*— . . . well, I wouldn't know," he said.

"That's what I heard." For over 20 years Paco has claimed that there *are* no political prisoners in Spain. Only "common criminals."

We met one of these common criminals within two weeks of our arrival. In fact, he had lived in our hotel for awhile and was employed somewhere in Barcelona. We had heard about him before we met; he had been one of the innumerable Spaniards who filled the gaps in the ranks of the International Brigades after April 1938. After the war was lost, he did something utterly incredible: he hid in a house for seven years! (Anyone who would do a thing like *that*, must have been a most *un*common criminal.)

After he surfaced, thinking it was safe, he was picked up by the police—and given a five-year prison sentence. They said he had been a Communist (of course), but in 1967 he still seemed to be a patently frightened man* who kept his opinions (if any) to himself. He did not enter into the hot political discussion in the bar of the hotel that afternoon, but he watched each speaker carefully and he made me very uncomfortable.

Spain is full of common criminals and we met them every day. We did not get into a taxicab without asking how things went—and we were told. We were told in expletives and in the imaginative obscenities the Spanish have developed over centuries of class oppression and anticlericalism.

Taxis provide the cheapest rides in Spain today and most of them are bought and paid for by their drivers. No cabman works less than 16 hours a day and for the one who told us he

---

* This was a snap judgment, I'm afraid. Two months after our return home I received a column from a weekly magazine published in Barcelona, which contained a short article about the blacklisted film artists of Hollywood. It was quite outspoken in its admiration for these men and although it was signed only with his initials, it indicated that he was far from being frightened into silence.

was doing "fine" on 700 *pesetas* a day ($10 then), 30 told us they took in no more than 450, when they earned that much. Out of it they made their monthly payments, bought gas and oil and tires, paid for repairs if they could not make them themselves, paid for insurance and for servicing and maintenance, and, if married, could not make it unless their wives and children also worked. (These men are aristocrats, of course. The average worker in factory or farm earned about 100 *pesetas* a day in 1967. The daily minimum wage was 96 *pesetas*.)

If you asked their opinion of Paco or the government, the least they did was spit. Then they apologized to *la señora* for the obscenities that accompanied the gesture. But talk is cheap and action more indicative. Here are a few small facts which show which way the wind is blowing and demonstrate that the rain in Spain does *not* stay mainly in the plain.

Strikes, of course, are illegal but they have plagued the regime since 1941. Since 1965 they have mounted in intensity, in daring and in scope. They are based on current issues, not the issues of the war of 1936-1939. They reflect the chronic inflation of the economy; a cost of living that had risen 65 percent since 1959; an unfavorable balance of trade, despite the floods of tourist dollars and American industrial investment that accounted for almost half the foreign capital influx; the fight of workers for trade-union and political rights, for decent wages, hours and conditions. The "legal" working day is eight hours but management exacts ten to twelve with no overtime, and the authorities look the other way. If you don't like it, you can go elsewhere and, as Anatole France observed the year that I was born: "The law, in its majestic equality, forbids all men to sleep under bridges, to bed in the streets, and to steal bread—the rich as well as the poor."

In January 1967 100,000 workers demonstrated in Madrid. Students joined them, shouting, "Students are with the workers; police are with the bankers!'' There was a two-hour pitched battle, 500 were arrested and the next day 30,000 more demonstrated in the streets against the arrests; then, in succeeding days, 55,000 in Madrid, 15,000 in the Asturias, 12,000 in Barcelona, thousands in Sevilla—and the prisoners were released! (Something new had been added.)

Writing in the *National Guardian* (New York) on 25 February 1967 Alvarez del Vayo, last foreign minister of the Spanish Republic, quoted a Madrid attorney who had been a guest at the American Embassy as saying, ''It is fantastic! They (the American officials) are the only ones who do not realize that a revolutionary process has begun in this country.'' (Does that remark strike an echo with what we know about official American understanding—in quotation marks—of what went on in Vietnam for decades?)

On April 15th (still 1967) workers in Bilbao struck and the students supported them again. Priests supported them too, and there was increasing evidence that the lower echelons of the Spanish Church—and now, elements of the hierarchy itself—were split, with parish priests being regularly arrested and beaten as brutally as any worker.

In May of the same year the universities of Madrid and Barcelona were closed by the government, with armed police occupying both campuses—but not before the students had made it plain what they felt: they ripped down photographs of Franco on the classroom walls, just as on April 28th they had held anti-Vietnam war demonstrations, burned the American flag and an effigy of Lyndon Baines Johnson.

On May Day itself there had been anti-U.S. and anti-Vietnam war demonstrations in Madrid, Barcelona, Bilbao, Salamanca and many other cities. ''Yankee, Go Home!'' was heard this time in Spain, just as there are similar slogans written on walls today in every country of Europe, North Africa, Latin America and Asia.

The headlines alone sometimes tell the story: these are from the *New York Times*: October 21, 23, 26, 27 and 28 (1967) respectively:

UNIONS' RESTIVENESS
INCREASING IN SPAIN

SPAIN DETAINS 31
TO CURB PROTESTS

MORE LABOR CHIEFS
ARRESTED BY SPAIN

Spain Warns Labor Against Demonstrating Today

PROTESTS CHECKED
BY SPANISH FORCES

Rebellion Against Regime Erupts Again in Madrid

The warnings and the arrests have done no good. The demonstrations and the underground work continue. Hundreds of arrests and dismissals of workers have taken place since that October 28th, when there were massive demonstrations which cemented the unity of the workers and the students.

The first week we were in Barcelona there was a demonstration in Tarrasa, a few kilometers from the city. The reports were conflicting: it was said that someone had thrown a hand grenade (or a rock) at a police jeep (no one was injured); others said that only rocks were thrown.

For three days the town was entirely surrounded by police, *Guardia Civil* and army; house-to-house search was made for anyone who might possibly have been involved in the affair. More than 200 were arrested.

Not one word about this small action appeared in any Barcelona paper and the next day the international edition of the *Herald-Tribune* did not arrive on the newsstands. (This happened about two or three times a week and the very next

day we invariably got the news of what had been going on.)
But everyone in Barcelona had heard of this action in Tarrasa
within hours after it happened—some, from people arriving in
town, others from listening to a clandestine Spanish radio,
broadcasting from—Czechoslovakia.

Selected items, however, which reflect the situation—in
the way the regime *wants* it reflected (shades of U.S. news
reports about the U-2 "incident," the Bay of Pigs fiasco,
Guatemala, the Gulf of Tonkin "attack," the daily events in
Vietnam, the *Pueblo* "spy-ship" episode in North Korean
waters)—*do* appear regularly in the Spanish press.

Nothing about the mass demonstrations, of course, but
here are three items from the *Vanguardia Española* of 17
December 1967 (all from Madrid):

Two Trials for Illegal Demonstration and Propaganda
   (Four years, two months and one day and 50 thousand *pesetas* for
   one defendant; six months, one day and 10 thousand *pesetas* for
   the second)

Three Years of Prison for Illicit Association
   (Here was a case right out of the Resnais-Semprun film called *La
   Guerre est Finie*—which demonstrated that the war is very far
   from being over. It involved a Spaniard and a Frenchman who
   were caught entering Spain at La Junquera, "and who were attempting to introduce into our country various copies of the newspaper *Mundo Obrero*, organ of the central committee of the
   Communist Party, as well as other printed matter and leaflets of
   works by Lenin and Carlos Marx. Three years of prison for each,
   and fines of 25,000 *pesetas* "for the use of false identification
   papers.")

Priest Condemned

This last was also pretty cute. It seems that Don Domingo
González Martínez de Montoya of the diocese of Bilbao was

accused, tried and condemned for having "distributed to various bookstores in the said capital, during last April, a number of copies for sale of a work of which he was the author, entitled 'God . . . On Strike?' "

For not having submitted this book to the proper authorities, he was found guilty of "clandestine printing" and sentenced to three months in prison, "with its accessories, suspension of all public activities, his profession, office and right to vote, and payment of all costs."

In 1846 a British traveler named Richard Ford published a book called *Gatherings from Spain*, in which he told the following lovely story, many versions of which may still be heard today throughout the Iberian peninsula:

When Ferdinand III captured Seville and died, being a saint he escaped purgatory, and Santiago presented him to the Virgin, who forthwith desired him to ask any favours for beloved Spain. The monarch petitioned for oil, wine and corn—conceded; for sunny skies, brave men, and pretty women—allowed; for cigars, relics, garlic, and bulls—by all means; for a *good government*—"Nay, nay," said the Virgin, "that can never be granted; for were it bestowed, not an angel would remain a day longer in heaven."

During the war that story was current and it surely applies today. In 1873 the first Spanish Republic was proclaimed, and after 11 months it was overthrown—by the generals, of course.

In the sixth and seventh editions of his *Leaves of Grass*, Walt Whitman, saluting the temporarily defeated republicans, published a new poem. Its second and last stanza reads:

> *Nor think we forget thee maternal;*
> *Lag'd'st thou so long? shall the clouds*
> *close again upon thee?*

Ah, but thou hast thyself now appear'd to us—
    we know thee,
Thou hast given us a sure proof, the glimpse of
    thyself,
Thou waitest there as everywhere thy time.

III

"You started something . . . Papa . . ."

1

If you cannot speak, read or write the language, it is difficult to know what is going on. If you have the money to spend, you will not notice how few people can enjoy the almost faultless food at the Basque restaurant called *Guria*, where the service is also unobtrusive and impeccable.

You will see the shops on the Diagonal and Paseo de Gracia which are crammed with luxury goods whose prices compare almost exactly with our own. There are custom tailors with British names like Gales and custom hatters with Catalan names like Prats—and how many people in any time or place have ever had a hat or even a suit made to order?

The rich live very well indeed but you only see them on the main boulevards and in the *lujo* hotels, restaurants and stores, and while there are many *Mercedes* in town that are newer and cleaner than the one Pipo drove, the majority of the cars racing madly through the streets and down the alleys at all hours of the day and night are antique *Citroëns* and the cheap Spanish version of the Italian *Fiat* called a *Seat*, both of which are controlled and partly owned by General Motors.

But Spain is still largely an agricultural country and the majority of its workers in field, factory or even in the offices do not drive *Seats* or eat at *Guria* or even at such (relatively) inexpensive places as *La Puñalada* or *SanSiro* or *Los Caracoles*.

Consider for a moment the privileged workers of the internationally glamorous motion picture industry. In 1967, an extra player, who must supply his own wardrobe (except in costume pictures) earned between 200 and 500 *pesetas* ($2.80

to $7.10) for a day that can begin (as one such day began when Camino started shooting) at four in the afternoon, and end at five the next morning.

Such a role as "Dr. Thompson," the American brain surgeon who accompanies the protagonist to Barcelona—a comedy-relief character who appears in several scenes and is what an American actor would call "a juicy little part"—was budgeted at 20,000 *pesetas* ($285) for three weeks' work.

Stars? The best-known *Spanish* motion picture stars then earned as much as $5,000 for a job that can take three months to complete. Even the director got more than that; Camino's contract called for $10,000 for the best part of a year's work, for he also prepared the production in every detail (something a producer or even a unit manager does in the United States), cast it, scouted locations, directed the shooting, edited it and supervised the dubbing and the scoring.

Who, then, are the rich? They are the very same people who lived very well indeed before the war: the owners of the *latifundia*, the great estates; the manufacturers whose enterprises in many instances are nothing more than masked subsidiaries of American cartels (oil and electric power, machinery and construction, automobiles and aluminum, telephone and telegraph); the Spanish Catholic Church, which recovered all its vast commercial and agricultural holdings.

They are the beneficiaries of the more than two billion dollars we (U.S. banks and military establishments) had invested at that time, and which had created something new for Spain—a corrupt middle class that rides around in *Mercedes-Benz* limousines that cost them $8,000 apiece (twice what the same model then cost in the United States).

Then, of course, there are the floods of American dollars that have poured into the country since Spain became a tourist "Paradise" after 1953. Very little of the new wealth of this American colony has "trickled down" to the average Spanish citizen, and his paradise is becoming more expensive for him every day, just as the average Vietnamese saw nothing of the billions in "aid" we poured into that wretched land. It sticks to the right fingers, however (meaning *right*).

Yet in Barcelona the complete *pensión* at a class IA hotel like the Majestic still cost about 600 *pesetas*—$10 when we arrived; $8.57 when we left. ("Have you heard the latest news? Franco's going to get the Nobel Prize for Chemistry." "Is that so? Why?" "He's just converted the *peseta* into a shit.")

DOCTOR TOMAS (Dr. Foster is listening): It's like the story of the milkmaid, only in reverse. . . . If the tourist trade fell off, everything would come to a head. Pay close attention. To begin with, they would close certain hotels and, naturally, they would build fewer apartment houses. What would that mean? It would mean unemployment for cooks, waiters, building workers and all those people who, in one way or another, live on the tourist trade. Are you following me? This means that these people, without work, would buy less clothing, footwear, fewer television sets, less wine. . . . In a word, their level of consumption would fall. With this—and here comes the chain reaction—there would be a crisis in the shoe industry, the clothing industry, the manufacture of wine and all the rest. And if the tourist industry falls off, we are . . .*

*

It became apparent from the first week that we were going to be there longer than the three weeks covered by the *Air France* ticket I had received, and Jaime agreed that this was so. He gave my three-week excursion ticket to the other

---

* This speech, of course, was deleted by the censor, but the Spanish newspapers sometimes print the truth—obliquely: MADRID, 16 December—The world tourist trade, which in 1966 involved 150,000,000 people and a world monetary total of $113 billion, brought to our country — as a host-country for tourists — the sum of $1.245 billion . . .

La Vanguardia, 17 December, 1967

Jaime and said it would be exchanged for an "open" ticket immediately, and returned to me.

It seemed that I was needed to "perfect" the scenario, as he had written me, to advise him about the character of the American doctors, to translate into good American English the dialogue written in Spanish for the three American characters, to write whatever new scenes occurred to me—for his inspection and approval.

Now he also wanted me to translate *all* the dialogue, so that good American English would appear in subtitles (if the film was sold abroad). It was impossible, of course, to translate all the dialogue until all the dialogue had been written and approved by him and by Román, in conference. And this was made more difficult by the fact that new dialogue was being written daily, by both Jaime and by me; Román was now employed on another job—not as a screenwriter, but as an editor and writer on a new encyclopedia—and was therefore not as available to either of us as he should have been.

I began to beef about the extra time involved, the extra work. Sylviane and I had worked out a careful itinerary for the two months we could afford to be abroad. It included a week's visit in Perpignan to see her relatives (exiles from Algeria), a two-week visit to her former home, Morocco (many cities of which I wanted to see, in addition to Casablanca), a possible visit to East Berlin where I had some blocked currency in the form of royalties from the third German edition of *The un-Americans* and a television play, and certainly at least a week in Paris.

I also beefed about the money, for there was to *be* no money aside from the transportation and living expenses. Jaime agreed with me that I was being exploited, both by him and by *Pandora Films*. I did not mind being exploited by *him*, I said, because he was certainly one of the most *agradable* men I had ever met, and the job had given me an opportunity I had never expected to enjoy—a chance to see a little more of Spain.

He spread his hands and showed his dimples. "You must understand," he said, "that my bringing you here was one of my follies. The *Pandora* people in Madrid thought I must be crazy when I suggested the idea. 'What do we need an *American* for?' they asked me, and I had to argue for weeks until they said, 'O.K., we'll send him a ticket and expenses but that's *all* we'll do and we still think you're crazy.' Perhaps I am."

"Perhaps you're not," I said, "but *they* are crazy if they think I'll do all this extra work for nothing. After all—"

"I'll see what I can do," he said.

"You better *had*," I said, and translating literally into Spanish, I said, "No tickee, no washee."

"*Perdón?*" he said.

The conversation must have had some effect because three days later something new was added. Perhaps he had even been contemplating the thing before, because I had been disconcerted by the fact that he seemed to watch me with more than ordinary concentration—and had been doing it since we arrived.

At our first story conference Martha had also upset me by taking endless pictures of me in his office, from every sort of angle. On the trip to Tarragona and beyond the Ebro, she had done the same thing. Now the photographs appeared and one blowup of my head delighted Camino so much that he covered his diploma as professor of piano by slipping it into the frame. (She had taken lots of pictures of Sylviane, as well, but none of them ever seemed to be printed.)

He suddenly said, "You will play the role of Doctor Thompson."

After I had made certain that I understood what he had said (after all, it was in his rapid French that sounded more like Catalan, which he also spoke), I looked at him and said, "I'm not an actor."

"You told me you had done some acting on the stage."

"I told you," I said, "that *40 years ago* I worked on the New York stage as an extra and bit-player. I also told you I was a very *bad* actor. That's why I quit the stage."

"You also told me you were never unemployed for the four years you worked in the theater. You couldn't have been *so* bad."

"Forget it," I said. Then I had a bright idea. "Unless you want me to be the star. I would be *very* good as Doctor Foster."

He laughed and said, "Too old."

"Typecasting again! Why can't Foster be 63 instead of 53?"

"Because," he said, deadpan and with the bedroom eyes half-closed, "three reasons: One—you're too handsome for the role. Two—you cannot learn to speak the Spanish dialogue fluently in so short a time."

"He *has* to speak in Spanish?"

"*Claro*. And three—I've decided to hire an American actor you must know. You know, you saw him when we screened the Spanish western that he made, last week."

"Mark Stevens?" I said. "I don't know him."

"You wrote a picture he played in, in Hollywood."

"I did?"

"Of course," he said. "*Objective Burma*."

"I don't remember him," I said. "How come he speaks Spanish fluently?"

"He lives here. In Mallorca. He's lived here a long time. He owns a hotel there, I heard. Once in awhile he makes a picture."

"If you can get him, you can get another actor."

"*Imposible*. You must understand the financial problems of the Spanish industry. We can't afford to import an actor, even from Italy, even from France." He smiled. "But you are here."

"I told you, I'm not an *actor*. I can read lines intelligently—any intelligent person can—but when I stand up on my feet I don't know what to do with my arms, my legs or my body."

"*No importa*," Jaime said. "I will tell you what to do."

"I know De Sica and Fellini can get performances out of nonprofessionals, but—"

"I," said Jaime, "am the Spanish Fellini." He smiled again and so charming is his smile that I doubt there is anything he can ask from anyone under any circumstances that he cannot get.

Then he looked pathetic and said, "It's the only way I can get some extra money for you."

"How much?"

"The role is budgeted for 20,000 *pesetas*. I will ask for 40."

After a moment I said, "*Pandora*'s right. You *are* crazy."

"*Un poco*," he said. I said I would discuss it with Sylviane.

She flipped her lid. "Look," she said. "This blows our plans sky-high."

"I know."

"We were going to stay three weeks and it's almost three weeks now. When will this end?"

"Jaime says we start shooting November 25th and he can finish with me by the third of December."

"*If* he starts the 25th," she said. "*If* he finishes with you by the third. This is *Spain*. And when are you going to take something for your cold?"

"*Mañana*. Jaime says there are two ways to do it. We can start the 25th and be absolutely finished—with me, that is—the 10th of December."

"That's too late."

"Wait. Or we can work till the third of December and if some scenes with Thompson still have to be shot, then I can come back from Morocco the 17th and be positive of finishing the 23rd. And come back to Casablanca to spend Christmas with you, *en famille*."

"Who pays for all these tickets? *Pandora*?"

"We'll work it out," I said.

She looked at me carefully and said, "Do you *want* to do this?"

"It's a way to earn some extra money that will help cover *your* expenses."

"For some extra work. I asked if you *wanted* to do it."

"Not particularly," I said, then shyly, "but it might be fun."

"You *want* to do it," she said with a smile.

"Once a ham . . ."

"He won't *get* 40,000 *pesetas*, and—by the way—where's your airplane ticket?"

"Jaime says *mañana*."

"Which Jaime?"

"Both of them."

She sighed. "I'll tell you what. I was hoping you could get some time off to go to Perpignan again with me, but I think I'll go alone and spend four or five days."

Then she smiled again and said, "You're going to have to lay down the law, you know. You're going to have to tell Jaime that if you're not through by the third, that's *it*! We're going to Morocco and you're not coming back."

"*Seguro*."

"And stop speaking Spanish to me, *actor*," she said, and kissed me.

2

Since the train we had taken to Perpignan and back that first weekend was so uncomfortable, even if it was reasonably on time, I saw her off on a bus in the driving rain from the huge Plaza de la Universidad. Then I went back to the hotel and went to bed.

The thermometer I had insisted on bringing with us from California said, 102 degrees. It wasn't a simple cold, at that. I called Jaime and he appeared within half an hour with a man he introduced as Doctor Sanpons.

"Sanpons?" I said. "That name is quite familiar."

"There's a doctor by that name in the script," said Jaime, and Sanpons examined me. That is, he bent down to my chest and applied his ear to my heart. He had me sit up and thumped my back. He didn't even take my pulse.

I looked at him; he was a cadaverous looking man in his thirties who looked as though he might be dying of T.B. His hair was uncut and hung halfway down his neck. If *he's* a doctor, I thought, then I am Dr. William Mayo.

Sanpons sent up some medications from the pharmacy on the corner and the fever was gone the next morning. I stayed in bed and began to think of Dr. Thompson. If I was going to try to be an actor, I would do what my old friend Morris Carnovsky had told me *he* did, in preparing for a role. I tried to remember what I had read in Stanislavsky's *An Actor Prepares* 40 years before; I couldn't. So I read and reread the script.

Dr. Thompson was from Texas. Well, I had been in Texas once; in fact, I had spent a year there, with two months off for good behavior. I recalled Professor Irwin (The World's Foremost Authority) Corey's famous gag:

"Tonight we're going to give out prizes. The first prize is a week in Texas. The second prize is . . . *two* weeks in Texas."

The doctor appears in seven scenes, some short, some long. In three he says nothing; that leaves four. But in those four he has to be a character, someone who is *not* the man who plays him.

I began to make some notes—and write additional dialogue for the scenes he played with the protagonist ("Once a ham . . ."). Since David Foster was an antifascist who had fought in Spain as a doctor, Dr. Thompson could, naturally, be a reactionary. I expanded the scene between the two doctors that takes place during the airliner's arrival over Barcelona:

THOMPSON: Man, that's a beautiful city. And mighty large. Has it changed much?

DAVID: I don't know. I never saw it from the air.

THOMPSON: When did you see it last?

DAVID: I haven't been back since the war.

(So far, as written by Camino and Gubern)

THOMPSON: What made you come here in the first place?

DAVID (cool): I'm a surgeon . . . like you.

THOMPSON (amused): Oh, come off it, Dave. You had more practice in New York than you could handle, even in those days. You didn't have to run off to a crummy little war that was none of your business.

DAVID (sincerely, but reserved): Maybe I was crazy. Maybe I felt it *was* my business. I volunteered, like the rest.

FLASHBACK: Surgeons operating in a field hospital; perhaps a tent.

BACK TO SCENE

THOMPSON: You *must* have been crazy. Medicine and politics don't mix.

DAVID: So they keep telling me.

In Foster's room in the *Hotel Ritz* (a suite, we were told, that had been used by the last Alfonso when he was in town), another side of Thompson's character is revealed: the hard-boiled reactionary brain surgeon from Texas thinks bullfights are barbaric. That was good for a couple laughs.

He got two other laughs riding in a taxicab with David on their way to the Congress of Neuro-Surgeons, but these were the original writers' lines. As they pass Gaudí's *casa loca* on the Paseo de Gracia he refers to it as "wrinkled." As they pass the monument where Generalissimo crosses Gracia, he asks what it is and the newspaperman interviewing David Foster says, "It's the Obelisk of Victory."

"What victory?" says Thompson, then remembers, "Ah yes, Franco's victory."

Then, trying to build up my part, I had a bright idea for the last important scene he plays, in the lobby of the Ritz the night they leave for the good old U.S.A. He has been arguing (as Jaime and Román wrote it) with Foster about the time the Pan American jet will leave.

Since I had bought a *navaja* our first week in town, one of those marvelously sharp folding knives that are made in Albacete and which every one of the I.B. men had had during the war, I thought of a way to use it in the film.

Foster is bored stiff by Thompson and is trying to get away to the phone to locate the young María before she leaves for Sevilla and he leaves for New York. He needs to say good-bye—if nothing else. Thompson stops him, saying, "Hey, Dave, ah got something t' show you," and pulling the six-inch blade, which opens with the marvelous sound of a rachet, he says, "Ah got me a new scalpel!"

I wrote a memorandum for Jaime in my fluent, unidioma-

SPAIN AGAIN: (Dr. Foster, left, and Dr. Thompson): "Ah got me a new scalpel . . ."

tic French, concerning the character of Thompson—and was mildly amazed at how closely (although sometimes in reverse) it fit my own character:

1. He is ten years older than David and he looks it.
2. He might wear rimless glasses, or glasses with steel rims. (*He didn't; he wore my horn-rimmed glasses.*)
3. Although he is a surgeon he seems to be nervous all the time. He is worried about lots of things that are not important—what time it is, whether the plane will be late, what time it will take off, whether they will miss it, and so forth.
4. If David was, or still is, a man of the left, Thompson is a man of the right, without having any political affiliations whatsoever. He is very much afraid of what is called "socialized medicine," as we see it not only in the socialist countries, but also in England.

5. He might possibly be a "camera nut," and, like other tourists, he carries one all day long and is always trying to take pictures —from the plane, the taxi, walking through the streets. (*He carried the camera case, but there was no camera inside.*)
6. He might be almost a clown, with no sense of humor, but he must not steal the scene from Dr. Foster. (*Alehvai!*)
7. And he speaks with a Texas accent, which I cannot do very well." (*Understatement of the decade.*)

Jaime read these notes while I was still in bed and said, "*Muy bien.*" He looked at me and said, "You know, you photograph very well."

"Martha is a very good photographer," I said. He nodded.

"Speaking of photographers," I said, "how did you make out with that gorgeous Finn?"

He made a face I have been trying vainly to duplicate ever since, but you have to have the sort of mustache that he wears and no doubt the structure of his face has something to do with it as well. He puffed out his lower lip and the mustache bristled. He popped his eyes. There are some things that cannot be described, but the total effect provided an answer to any unanswerable question.

"She told me to call her when I got to Hollywood. I did. In ten minutes she was at my hotel with an enormous Cadillac. She handed me the keys and told me to drive to her apartment. In the car she started to put her hands on me and I said, 'Not so fast, please.' "

"In English or Spanish? Sounds like fun."

"Spanish. No fun. She was built marvelously but, you know, you can't keep that up all night. It was horrible. She wouldn't let me sleep."

"Poor Camino! And you were only 28 years old."

"Nothing to do with age. I'm a Spaniard."

*

Sylviane returned from four days in Perpignan saying, "You see, the minute I go away, you get sick."

"I was sick before you left."

"Do you start shooting the 25th?"

"No, the 27th."

I knew it," she said. I showed her the ancient map of northern Spain that I had brought from home. It was patched with Scotch Tape but it was quite detailed.

"Look," I said, "I've searched Gerona province for days and there *is* no Santa Coloma de las Planes."

"You were probably misinformed."

"But there *is* a Santa Coloma-de-*Farnés* . . . about 18 kilometers from Gerona."

"Let's rent a car and go there."

"What point is there? It would probably be a wild-goose chase."

"You won't be happy till you find him."

"I'm not so sure I'll be happy if we do. What do I *do*—take a picture of the grave for his father and mother? How would *you* feel if you suddenly got a picture of your son's grave . . . the son you lost 29 years ago?"

"You may be right," she said and we dropped the subject, for shooting started Monday in the *Ritz*. I had written all the new scenes I could think of and most had been accepted, but there had been no time to incorporate them all into the revised script that Jaime handed me.

"I have to think of some of these," he said.

"I'll bet you do."

"Some I may rewrite myself."

I had even managed to translate half of all the dialogue before we started, and Jaime said there was no need to do the rest until I was home in California.

The first scenes in Dr. Foster's hotel room were supposed to start at nine that morning and I had received from Jaime *el Cid* an official piece of paper that was delivered to the hotel to *Señor Don Betsi*, and was called a *Citación*. It said I would be picked up at 8:30 a.m. at my *domicilio* by a car, and that I was to wear the white shirt, dark gray suit, the striped necktie.

Now, that was something, wasn't it? I wasn't sure whether Robert Taylor was driven to work in a limousine, but I knew that Bette Davis and John Garfield drove their cars onto the Warner Brothers' lot, way back in 1943.

Promptly at 8:30 a.m. (amazing!) a chauffeured car arrived at the hotel and drove me to the *Ritz* on the Avenida of that other *puto*, José Antonio Primo de Rivera, the Patron Saint of the *Falange*. Sylviane was awake but she was not kindly disposed to the idea of watching the shooting at such an ungodly hour. "You won't start on time," she said, and as usual, she was right. We did not start till one that afternoon.

This gave me time for several things: to study my lines, which I was not at all sure I could remember; to watch the lighting of the bedroom, with equipment that seemed about as primitive as the kind they used in Hollywood for the Mack Sennett comedies.

They took lights down and put them up. They hung them from an iron pole stretched from wall to wall; it promptly fell down. They made reflectors out of large sheets of white paper that they tacked on the walls and ceiling with thumbtacks. They had cables with male terminals that did not fit the female terminals. And when everything was ready for the first scene there was a brilliant short circuit, the curtains on the windows under the pole on which the lights were hanging caught fire and everyone went mad.

I had met the star before, at Jaime's house. My name meant nothing to him—which somewhat miffed me, for I had thought that with all the publicity between 1947 and 1950 when we went to jail, *everyone* (especially in The Industry) knew all about the nefarious Hollywood Ten.

He had been very pleasant when we met and he had remembered *Objective Burma*, saying, "It's the first picture I ever worked in."

I felt compelled to confess to him that I had done very little acting and all of it on the stage, and I said, pitiably, "You'll have to help me."

"Gladly," he said. "There's nothing to it."

"I don't think I can do the Texas accent very well," I said, and he promptly launched into an extemporaneous speech in an excellent Texas accent that curled me green with envy. When he was called away by the wardrobe lady, I went into the Roman bathroom of the suite, locked the door and tried to imitate him as best I could. My best was no good at all.

(There was a marvelous sign on a small plastic plaque fastened to the wall, that read—in four languages: *Important: Never use the telephone while taking your bath.* For some reason or other it reminded me of another sign I had seen in a public bathhouse in Paris in 1928. It was a "family" bathroom with two tubs and a curtain that could be drawn between them. The sign on the wall read: *It is forbidden to get into the same tub.*)

By the time Sylviane arrived, she was just in time to witness the progressive humiliation of her husband, for I had told Camino the literal truth: I *didn't* know what to do with my hands or feet or body.

I had been telling myself something I had even learned in Hollywood, without the benefit of watching films by Fellini or De Sica: you do not *need* to be an actor to work in film. You don't. (But it helps.) Granted the ability to read lines, all you have to do is precisely what the director tells you. You do not step beyond the chalk-marks on the floor that indicate where you are to stand. You do not turn your body further than you need to, nor your head, because if you do you pop out of the frame. You do not need to "project," either your personality or your voice, for the microphone picks up a whisper and the camera exaggerates everything you do to the point where what may seem to you a simple wink turns out to look like a case of cerebral palsy.

All that was required of me in that first scene was to knock on the bedroom door, enter, notice that Dr. Foster was on the phone, indicate (with my face) that I had noticed it, and move quietly into the room and wait for him to hang up and say, "What's up, Thompson?"

After the wardrobe lady had brushed my suit and shined my shoes 15 times and I had knocked, entered, seen Foster, made a face and moved into the room (15 times), I was drenched with perspiration and felt as though I had played Lady Macbeth's sleep-walking scene at the Metropolitan Opera House before 3,000 madly jeering customers.

That is when you find out that the films are *really* a director's medium, for Camino finally gave up trying to get me to move and turn correctly, and told me to stand perfectly still before the mirror, my back to Dr. Foster on the bed, and deliver all my lines into the glass.

This worked, and when Foster rose and moved into the closet for some clothes, I was covered by his movement so that the next shot could discover me seated in the armchair, to deliver the rest of my lines without falling over my feet.

We did that scene over and over and over and then we did a silent, *solo* scene of Dr. Thompson pouring good bourbon whiskey into two glasses full of ice and carrying them out of the room. Then we did the bathroom scene.

I would give my left arm and five years of my waning life to have such a bathroom, but you can't have everything. It was a Roman bathroom and Jaime devised some "business" for his nonactor:

After delivering the whiskey to Dr. Foster, who was

shaving with my electric razor because his electric razor had a European plug and mine had a transformer (realism!), Dr. Thompson looks at the Roman bath and *walks down into it* with whiskey glass and cigarette in hand, then starts talking about the bullfights.

It develops into an argument, and Thompson climbs out of the tub, fumbling the whiskey glass in one hand and the cigarette in the other, and continues the argument sitting on the toilet. He lifts the lid, still sitting, and deposits the cigarette butt, then, as Foster ends the argument and walks out of the bathroom, Thompson watches him, takes a swig of the bourbon—and the actor "playing" him forgot to swallow, then *tried* to swallow and nearly strangled.

This take looked very funny when we saw the rushes the next evening in a projection room in the film-processing laboratory, and it wouldn't surprise me if Camino left it in. (He did.) The whiskey-pouring and the Roman bath looked gorgeous in Glorious Eastmancolor.

We had done these scenes so many times that I was beginning to achieve some relaxation—out of sheer fatigue and simple *je-m'en-foutisme*—and that is how I learned the second important fact about motion-picture acting.

Anyone who wants to be a movie actor is insane, for there is no more boring profession on the face of God's still partly green earth. There are compensations, however—even if they don't exist in Spain. As the prison guard told me in Texarkana, Texas, when I asked him if he *liked* being a screw:

"Hell, no," he said, "but it's better than *working* for a living."

3

Excerpt:

(August 17, 1938) . . . Then it started again, and the echoes multiplied and reverberated among the peaks; it seemed miles

away, though it was only a few hundred meters at best. There would be a sudden, heavy explosion and a bright flower-pot of bursting flame as a mortar exploded; silence, the shouting and the subdued murmur; a few bullets cracked nearby and it was quiet. Alternately, every few minutes, this went on, then silence. Then it was silent for a long time and suddenly we were aware that there were men near us, coming by us silently, not very many men at first, but soon more and more of them, filling the emptiness around us with heavy breathing. Someone was sobbing. Someone said, "Help me, I'm wounded." Antonio was in front of me, he saluted and said, "La pistola del Comandante," and thrust the automatic into my hand. I grasped it; it was sticky, and I held it up and could see it was wet with something. "El Comandante?" I said, but Antonio was gone, and Sam was in front of me, breathing rapidly.

"Aaron's hurt," he said. "In the head. It's nothing. Don't get excited; take it easy; he'll be all right."

"Are you sure? Where is he?"

"They took him out; they got him out. Did you get his pistol? He said to give it to you to keep."

"Yes . . ."

I could see in the pale light that filtered from behind the streaming clouds that he was crying. I remembered that Aaron had told me about that day on the first hill, when Sam had finally found him, after thinking him lost in the attack, and had become hysterical.

"Take it easy," I said.

"Aaron's all right," he said. "I helped him walk a little way back. Did we take the hill? he said; I told him Yes; How's the company? he said; I told him Fine. He'll be all right," he said. "He'll be all right!"

—Men in Battle

We got lost trying to find the street that would take us out of Barcelona to the coast highway and I felt a certain satisfaction because Sylviane had insisted that she would do the driving. She had three reasons: (1) I had been so spoiled by our automatic shifts that I could no longer work a stick; (2) I did not understand the European shifts anyhow; (3) I was too emotional that day to drive safely. (Right? Right.)

When we finally reached the coast highway and started northeast, all the names came back again for I had ridden many trucks through Badalona, Masnou and Mataró (where one of the American hospitals had been located), Arenys-de-Mar, Calella and Pineda.

The Mediterranean was battleship gray and low clouds promised rain and there was wind. It was Sunday and there were few people on the streets of any town.

At Malgrat the highway turned inland and ran almost due north and the countryside was somewhat pleasant. There were well-cultivated fields (and few *Coca-Cola* signs); there were manor houses set apart in the fields; there were those marvelous pines that seem characteristic of Spain. Their needles are very dark and their branches do not flower until the trunk has reached a considerable height.

We crossed a small river, and following my ancient map and the one supplied by Avis Rent-a-Car (*Nos esforzamos mas*) turned left at Sils on the road through Riudarenas to Santa Coloma-de-Farnés. These were small towns and it was astonishing to see, again, that plowing was still done with wooden plows, just as it had been during the war—and since the Middle Ages.

Each small town was introduced to and said farewell to the traveler through the *Falange* symbol standing beside the road and each small town—just like those on the Mediterranean littoral—was built to a pattern, with the Church and manor house, both of heavy stone, dominating a huddle of miserable brick and adobe houses, just as they have done since the Middle Ages.

Santa Coloma was larger than most of these towns, but

just as dismal. "A good place to be dead," I heard myself say. Sylviane agreed.

There was scarcely anyone on the streets, but we found someone to direct us to the town cemetery, just outside the most populated area, and reached it in a driving drizzle that was not heavy enough to be uncomfortable.

The iron gates of the cemetery were open and in the hour or more we spent there we saw only one other human being —an aging woman placing flowers before a tomb.

I was thinking, I don't know if I can stand this, especially if we find the grave. I don't know what's going to happen now. I could hear him saying—and I could *hear* his voice—"Keep your head down, Papa, or your kids will need another father." I could hear him say, "Wolff's after me to get a Spanish *ayudante*, and God knows you're useless except for organizing some tobacco now and then, but—"

I could see that lovely, ugly face, the soft dark-brown eyes, and hear the small but mellow voice as he sang *Home on the Range* to the accompaniment of a borrowed guitar that night during the rest period near Darnos. I could feel the warmth of his body next to mine, rolled in the same blanket inside the cave down in the *barranca* near Marsa.

His father has those eyes and they are so startling that, although the two men looked nothing alike (he looked like his mother), the eyes alone—when I called on the family in 1939 and saw them again in his father—made me think I was seeing Aaron. In 1967, in Los Angeles, one week before we left for Spain, they had had the same effect.

The graves were all above ground, cut into the walls of the cemetery itself, in tiers of three. We divided the cemetery between us and separated—for which I was grateful. I did not want my wife to see me fall apart again—as I had on the plane.

Most were obviously family tombs: they had stone or metal plaques which read *Familia González* or *Familia Pérez*.

Some had small, fading portraits of the long deceased in metal frames. A few had been visited recently and flowers had been placed in metal vases, attached to the wall itself.

Some had the names of the departed printed on the masonry that blocked the opening to the individual shelves on which the dead had been laid in coffins. Some of these names had been effaced by the wind, rain and sun of decades; some could be read, in part. Some had no names at all or had never borne them.

Sylviane and I met again in the middle of one wall. "Nothing," I said, with some relief, and she said, "I don't think he's here."

"Why not?"

"Look—this town is far off the beaten track. It's not even the shortest way to Gerona, if they were taking him that way en route to France. Why would he have been buried in such a godforsaken hole?"

"I wouldn't know."

We decided to speak to the old lady who was now leaving the cemetery and she told us that no doubt the *padre* would know who was buried there. Where could we find him, at the church? "No," she said, "he should be home for dinner at this hour," and pointed the direction we should take.

We drove up that way, then remembering that she had said he was a young priest, we decided he probably wouldn't know anything about 1938. Instead, we drove into the town and stopped at a corner where two men and a young boy in Sunday clothes were standing talking to each other.

We asked if there was anyone, a man who was in charge of the cemetery. Of course, they said, and one of the men said his *hijo* would show us where he lived and the bright-eyed lad of 12 or 13, wearing round eyeglasses, eagerly climbed into the car.

He directed us from one narrow, winding street into another until we figured he didn't know where he was going, but finally he pointed to a door. "He lives in there," the youngster said, and stayed in the car as we crossed the street and rang the bell.

Nobody answered, but it was not two minutes before a small crowd of people had assembled, seeing the rented car and the obvious foreigners. One man emerged in an undershirt and pants and *alpargatas* from a basement across the street. He was unshaved—and obviously plastered on his day off. Others came to the windows and looked out at us. The door next to the man's house opened and a youngish woman appeared and asked if we were looking for Señor José Turón.

The name amused Sylviane who said, "Turón like in *turrón*, the candy?" The woman laughed. She spoke in a regional dialect I found hard to understand. She had one black eye and, to our astonishment, she was shortly joined by a youngster (male) of maybe nine, who also had a blackened eye—the same one. (Maybe they smoked Tareyton cigarettes.)

She told us that Señor Turón was eating Sunday dinner in another town and probably wouldn't be back for quite awhile. Was there anything she could do for us?

Yes, we said. We were looking for the grave of a foreigner who was, we had heard, buried in the cemetery. We could not find his grave. Perhaps Señor Turón would have a list?

"*Claro*," she said. "When did the *extranjero* die?"

"In 1938," I said and the woman held one hand aloft and shook it at the wrist, as I had seen French people (including Sylviane) do many times.

"*Treinta-ocho!*" she said, as though we had said 400 years B.C.

"He was an American," we said. "Since we were travelling in Spain, we told his family we would try to find his grave."

"An American?" our little guide suddenly said (he had

come over from the car). *"De las Brigadas Internacionales?"*

"*Sí*," I said.

Well, the woman said, if he was a soldier—there had been so many people died in 1938. So many soldiers. Perhaps he had been buried in a common grave. (We had seen no signs of one.)

A man now appeared behind the woman and the child. He was unshaven, too, and had a smirk on his face. As long as we were there he stood and smirked—and said no word. (Neither of his eyes was blackened.)

We told the woman we would be grateful if she could find out anything from Señor Turón when he returned. We said we were leaving Spain soon for Morocco, but we gave our names and the name of our hotel in Barcelona. If she could find out anything perhaps we could return, take pictures of the grave for the man's family.

I could visualize the picture and it sickened me. We would find it and it would be untended, bare of any name (they all had numbers). We would paint the masonry, paint his name and dates of birth and death, clean up around it, place flowers in new metal containers on the wall—and send the color picture to his father and his mother in Los Angeles!

We thanked the woman, who was most gracious, and we left with our guide, offering to take him home. He told us where to go. I could hear a voice in my ear, saying, "What the hell're you doing, Papa? Shit, man, it was almost 30 years ago and you should have forgotten it. It's not *your* fault you didn't die instead of me."

I turned to the youngster in the back seat and said, "How does it happen that you know about the International Brigades?"

He looked surprised and somewhat hurt and said, "*Pues*, I read books."

"And what do the books tell you about the International Brigades?"

"That they were very bad men," the little boy replied.

"Do you believe that?" Sylviane said, from behind the wheel.

"*Claro.*"

I couldn't resist it, so I said, "Do *I* look like a very bad man?"

"Oh, no, no!" he said, the Spanish gentleman at thirteen. "Of course not." Then his eyes widened. "Were *you* a member of the International Brigades?"

"*Claro,*" I said with what I hoped was a gentle and paternal smile. "You will read many books," I added. "Some will tell you that they were very bad men. Some will tell you they were very good. When you're older, you will decide what is true and what is false."

We had arrived at his house and I offered him a few *pesetas* which he firmly refused until I put them in his pocket. Then he said, "*Muchas gracias.*"

On the road back to Riudarenas it started to rain and Sylviane said, "You know, you're a dope."

"Why?"

"Did you *have* to say you'd been in the Brigades?"

"Why not?"

"Because, *tonto*, you've been making such a secret of your presence here. Because we gave that woman our name and our hotel. Because you know the Brigade was considered Red. Because—"

"*Basta, mujer!*" I said, and then, "*Es igual.*"

"*Coño,*" said Sylviane. Then it started to rain with a vengeance and she squinted at the road as though it were 15 miles ahead of us. It came in a downpour like a cloud burst and the coast highway was flooded at points up to three and four inches of water.

"They sure don't know how to build roads here," she said. "The water doesn't run off—look at those people!"

There were people on the sidewalks in Calella who were

trying vainly to cross from one curb to another and were stranded. There were people trying vainly to cross the highway to the other side. The Mediterranean was whipped into leaden waves with foam on top of them. The wind shoved the car from side to side and cars passing us in both directions, with and without their lights, threw up sheets of water that drenched the windshield.

"*Na din moc!*" Sylviane shouted at a truck that had just passed and blinded us. She slammed on the brakes and we skidded sideways till the windshield was clear; then she started up again.

"*Na dil bebek!*" she cried.

4

My wife and I have had a running argument for years. She insists that after more than 20 years in the United States she is forgetting how to speak or write in French. I have argued that it is impossible to forget your native tongue, but this trip proved her point for she frequently lapsed from French into English or Spanish, and vice versa.

It also proved the converse of her theory; she told me the first year we were married that in her dreams her parents —who did not speak a word of anything but French, Spanish or Arabic—had suddenly begun to speak to her in English.

Now I was one up on her! After only four weeks in Europe, after one long weekend in Perpignan trying to communicate with relatives, after speaking Spanish and French to Camino and his associates, I had my first dream—in Spanish.

It was an argument with Jaime about the script and my Spanish was absolutely fluent and idiomatically correct. (In waking life I frequently started a sentence in Spanish and ended it in French, or vice versa.)

I wish I could remember that argument, for it was far more vehement than any we had had in conference. I cannot imagine the man ever raising his voice or growing angry, though I am reasonably certain he can do both.

The conferences were over now, for he was shooting —except when something went wrong and he called for one and I went to his apartment on appointment.

Generally he was late and the part-time housekeeper let me in and I sat in his workroom waiting, or examined his books. All my life I have had a compulsion common to most literary characters: I am compelled to read *anything* written or printed on paper, whether it is on a matchbook, the wrapping of a can of tuna or a roll of toilet paper.

Therefore I have always been an inveterate snoop who enjoys reading (or rather *must* read) other people's mail, so long as it is not in an envelope—*that* would be *infra dig*. Which explains why I noticed the typewritten sheet on his desk the moment I came in that afternoon.

There was no printed letterhead. There was no signature, but it was obvious from the first sentence that it was the list of objections the *Censura* in Madrid had sent to him— concerning the original script.

I wondered whether that was the way they usually did it—so no one could ship it out of the country or even make a photocopy that would make the censorship ridiculous.

Some objections were *so* ridiculous as to be hilarious:

• "Likewise the English title (*Spain Again*) should be changed to a Spanish title, otherwise the film will receive no protection whatsoever because of the confusion that could be produced concerning its nationality." (!)

• "In the production of the film anything should be sedulously avoided which, in an explicit or implicit manner, can create a reference or interpretation of our war which does not have an absolutely integral character, as well as the presentation of negative aspects of present-day Spanish life to those who might, in the context of the work, draw undesirable conclusions." (*Syntax and grammar as in the original.*)

Remembering that I had been told that all Spanish films were subsidized up to 60 percent of the cost of production—*if* they were approved—the operation of the carrot and the club was beautifully exemplified.

• "Consequently and in order not to incur (under Norm 13, 3a) anything which might bring about the prohibition of (*the film*), the production should pay particular heed to the following suggestions:

• "In the selection of scenes from the (*film*) archives, it should always be kept carefully in mind whatever negative effect might be produced on the spectator, whether by images on the screen or by montage.

• "Suppression of visual and verbal reference to the Obelisk of Victory . . ." (*There goes my laugh! But why? Weren't they proud of Franco's victory–or did they think someone in the theater might laugh when it was mentioned?*)

• "Suppression of Dr. Tomas' discourse about tourism . . ." (*There goes some content!*)

• "Suppression of the allusion to the disemboweled woman . . ." (*In Manuel's tavern, during talk about the bombing of the city.*)

• "Suppression of Manuel Sr.'s statement about 'so many died . . . so many dead . . .' " (*Only a million died and everybody knows it and the same novelist who wrote* The Cypresses Believe in God *wrote a second novel called* One Million Dead.)

• "Suppress the priest's remarks about 'the rich alumni . . . (*who were worse than the priest's students in the Academy of Science*) . . . and (*the man*) who wanted to study to be an engineer' (*but was driving a taxi in the city*), also, 'Yes, she had a hard time after the war. The truth is we all had a hard time after the war . . .'

• "Change 'brigades' to 'forces' or some similar expression.

• "Be warned about the undesirable significance and character of the scenes in the *masía* (*where the pig is killed*) and in the town in ruins . . .

• "Among other things it will be desirable to make it very clear that María was born after her mother's marriage, in order to avoid any possible implication of incest, as well as avoiding carnal excesses in the erotic scene between David and María in the *Hotel Ritz* . . ."

What would happen, I wondered, when they read and/or saw the additional dialogue I had written to point up the scenes between David and Manuel Jr. and Sr.—about the war; the sequence with the priest, a man named Jacinto who had been a nurse in Dr. Foster's mobile hospital, to bring out the difference between Jacinto, who speaks of his old friend as a "materialist," and David himself; the scenes in Corbera (which came right out of my own experience) and in the mental institution.

It was about these last scenes that Jaime had called what was to be our last story conference. I suddenly recalled the testimony of the "friendly" witnesses in 1947, who had accused us (but sedulously avoided citing chapter and verse) of "slipping Communist propaganda" into Hollywood films. I wondered if that was what I was trying to do. (What I had *not* done had resulted in my expulsion from The Industry—for over 20 years!)

Was it or was it not true that for historically conditioned reasons there *were* two prevailing mental aberrations in Spain (and not in Spain alone): religious mania and the recognizable phobia called anti-Communism? If it was true, why could they not be shown? Was it Communist propaganda to show the truth? Was I attempting to "slant" a film by dealing with the *beatas*, whom we had seen in every church we visited: the

Cathedral in Barcelona, Tibidabo, the "poor man's church" in Gandesa?

Was the truth being distorted and "used" for a purpose because I had developed the man whom Sylviane had over-heard outside the asylum into a scene *inside* the hospital? What was the difference between truth and propaganda—if there was any? How is reality reflected in a motion-picture script?

SEQ. 32   INTERIOR INSTITUTION. DAY

—A brief montage, almost documentary in nature, of the first half-hour of David's and María's visit to the hospital. Silent. We may see a few demented faces of patients who are permitted to work around the halls, cleaning, sweeping, and so forth. A couple of the men approach David for cigarettes. María shows some apprehension, withdraws slightly. But notic-ing how gently David and the other doctors treat these people, her fear disappears and she watches with interest. Doctors show deference to David, ask him questions, and he answers. As they proceed from room to room (showing possibly the dining room, kitchen, laundry, and so forth) we see other faces of patients who are at work, or sitting in the common room, withdrawn. One does not answer any questions addressed to her by Dr. Iglesias (the director) or by David. María's sympathy for the woman is visible in her face. As they proceed from room to room, the nurse accom-panying them unlocks doors and locks them behind the group.

INT. PATIENT'S ROOM. DAY.

—A simple room with a cot, a chair, a desk, a Holy Picture on the wall. The visiting group consists of Dr. Iglesias, David, María and the nurse. The patient is sitting in a chair, rises when the group enters. He is startled.

DR. IGLESIAS (to patient):   Joaquin, this is Dr. Foster.

David extends his hand and Joaquin, a man about 50, takes it.

DAVID: Sit down, Joaquin.

Joaquin sits, obediently.

DAVID: How long have you been here, Joaquin?

JOAQUIN: Two weeks, doctor.

DR. IGLESIAS (aside to David & María):   Twenty-three years . . . he hid in a house for six . . .

DAVID: Two weeks. And what are you doing here?

JOAQUIN (fearfully): Hiding . . . the good Doctor Iglesias saved me.

María stands against the wall, watching Joaquin with fascination.

DAVID: That was good of him. What did he save you from?

JOAQUIN: The Reds. They want to kill me.

DR. IGLESIAS: Why should they want to kill you?

JOAQUIN: I fought against them. I killed many. They want revenge.

DAVID: But you won the war, Joaquin, didn't you?

JOAQUIN (apprehensively): Yes. But they're still here.

DR. IGLESIAS: Where?

JOAQUIN: They're everywhere . . . waiting . . . looking for me.

The SOUND of an airliner is HEARD overscene. Joaquin looks up with apprehension, gets up a moment, then starts to hide under the bed.

JOAQUIN (fearfully): Planes! . . . Get *down*!

Dr. Iglesias takes the man's arm so he cannot hide under the bed. He speaks quietly to him.

DR. IGLESIAS: It's only an airliner, Joaquin. There's nothing to be afraid of.

JOAQUIN (trembling): They're coming to get me . . . (points at Dr. Iglesias) . . . they'll get you, too . . .

DISSOLVE TO

A HALLWAY. INSTITUTION. DAY.

   —David, María, the nurse and Dr. Iglesias have just emerged from Joaquin's room.

DAVID: What have you done for him, Doctor?

DR. IGLESIAS: We've tried everything. Hypnotism, psychotherapy, shock treatments, drugs . . . nothing helps. It's an obsession . . .

DAVID (thoughtfully): An obsession . . . yes.

Well, was it an obsession or wasn't it? Had not this same obsession forced the late James Forrestal, America's first Secretary of Defense, to leap from his hospital window to his death in 1949? Hadn't the creation of this obsession, its operation and manipulation, made it possible for Mussolini to save Italy; for Hitler to save Germany; for Franco to save Spain; for

Tojo to save Japan and half of China; for all of them, combined and determined, to save the human race, to murder millions? Wasn't it used by us to save Vietnam from the Vietnamese and won't it be used, if we give them half a chance, to save the U.S.A. from the Americans? If we do nothing to stop it, might we not see an American fascism established in the name of law and order and anti-Communism, and all dissent about foreign or domestic policies crushed because it gives "aid and comfort to the enemy"?*

"Román and I discussed this scene," Camino said. "We like it."

"I'm glad."

"But we cannot shoot it. We can shoot the second."

"Why not? I told you about the man we overheard outside the institution. He's *there*."

"You know the answer," Jaime said. "It would not be accepted."

I knew the answer so I did not argue. He was right. It would not be accepted.

"The second is all right?"

"Except for the last line," he said.

—Now the group enters a small waiting room where there is another nurse standing behind a chair in which a young girl about 24 is seated. She is somewhat pretty, rises immediately when the group enters and shakes hands with each as they are introduced by Dr. Iglesias.

GIRL: My name is Teresa. I was named after the Saint.

DAVID: Please sit down, Teresa.

---

* "NEW YORK—Former President Eisenhower said yesterday that he would withhold support from any candidate who advocates a pull-out from Vietnam, and he accused militant peace groups of 'rebellion' and near-treason. In an article in the April issue of Reader's Digest, Mr. Eisenhower accused war dissenters of giving 'aid and comfort to the enemy' . . ." (*San Francisco Chronicle*, quoting *N.Y. Times*, March 27, 1968).

—Teresa is at all times completely cheerful, almost happy, and although what she says makes no sense at all, she says it with complete conviction.

DR. IGLESIAS: Did you have any good talks today, Teresa?

TERESA (slightly disappointed):   Only one.

DAVID: Whom did you talk to?

TERESA: My Saint.

DAVID: Saint Teresa . . . what did she say?

TERESA: What she always says . . . to be a good girl . . . (Laughs, points at Dr. Iglesias). She said the doctor was a saint, too.

DR. IGLESIAS: I'm flattered. Did you believe her?

TERESA: Of course.

DAVID: You talk to other saints, too?

TERESA (simply):   Of course.

DR. IGLESIAS: Which ones?

TERESA (counts on her fingers):   St. Catherine, St. Anne, the Holy Saint Michael . . . the Blessed Virgin (crosses herself) . . .

DAVID: Do you speak to her often?

TERESA: Not often. She's very busy, you know. But I speak to my father every day.

DR. IGLESIAS (aside, to David & María):   He died three months ago.

DAVID: Is he a saint?

TERESA: Of course . . . of course, he has not been canonized yet but the Holy Father knows about him . . .

DAVID: Joan of Arc also spoke to these saints . . .

TERESA: Yes. She speaks to me, too. She told me last week that if I am a good girl, God may send me an angel, so I may accomplish my mission . . .

DR. IGLESIAS: What is your mission, Teresa?

TERESA: To save Spain for God.

"What's wrong with the last line?" I asked, and Jaime smiled.

"I have a better one," he said.

"Yes?"

"She puts one finger to her lips and says, 'It's a secret.' "

"I'll buy that," I said.

"*Perdón?*"

"A Hollywood expression," I said.

"I understand," said Jaime. "Very good."

"Speaking of Hollywood, how did the tests with The Girlfriend come out?"

He made that face again. "Very bad," he said. "She cannot act."

I had not seen any of her acting, but during the shooting of the bedroom scene between the two doctors she had been under the tender, loving care of two makeup women who quite literally spent three hours making up her striking face while a *duenna* who accompanied her at all times when The Boyfriend was not in town sat and watched.

"You knew that in advance, didn't you?"

"No. You have done very little acting, but you can act."

"You flatter me."

"I tell the truth," he said with a sad smile. "You saw the rushes; everybody laughed."

"They were laughing *at* me; not with me."

"*No importa*," said Jaime. "It was a character. It was amusing. It was what it was supposed to be."

"You're the Fellini of Spain," I said. "María is *your* problem."

"*Seguro*. When are you going to Casablanca?"

"If you're through with me—as far as you can go by Friday night—we'll take the bus to Perpignan Saturday morning, come back Sunday night and catch the early plane to Madrid on Monday. But where's my airplane ticket?"

"Before you leave—for certain."

"You've been saying that for almost five weeks!"

"I'm surrounded by incompetents," he said. "I had to fight for weeks to get the money to *start* the production."

"What's the matter with this *Pandora* anyhow?"

SPAIN AGAIN: "Is she as good as that fat dame, Maruja?"

"They don't understand what's involved in making a film."

"What *do* they understand?"

"Export-import."

"If I don't get the return ticket to San Francisco, I don't come back to finish the other scenes."

"I'll try," he said. Then, as I rose to leave he said, "We're rehearsing the *tablao flamenco* sequence Friday night. You can see her dance."

"That will be nice," I said. "Is she as good as that fat dame Maruja we saw at Los Tarantos in the Plaza Real last week?"

He made that face again.

5

Time has a way of collapsing when you are overburdened
with activity, just as you discover that it is also possible to do
things you are incapable of doing, when you have to. (I had
discovered that 29 years earlier, during the war.)

It is therefore difficult to remember the sequence of
events that week before we left for Morocco, but visual and
sense impressions remain, so mixed up that it is impossible to
sort them out.

There was the time we were having a very good martini
in the hotel bar when that fellow who had hidden in a house for
seven years and then spent five in prison appeared with three
young men to whom we had been introduced one night in a
movie house.

All of them were in the motion-picture industry in one
capacity or another. Two or three were directors of
avant-garde films that we had seen, all of which were brilliantly acted, directed, photographed, edited and scored—and
not one of which made any sense at all. (Or very little sense.)

We had an argument about those films. We had an argument about the war in Spain that had ended when these young
men, the directors, were all of two or three years old. They
had very strong opinions about it, nevertheless.

Franco had made a speech to the Cortes on November
17th which I had clipped from *La Vanguardia* and was determined to read. Somebody told me about a magazine whose
publication had been suspended for three months, and whose
editor had been fired because of an article it had published,
and I had found a copy of that issue in the hotel lobby.

Someone else had handed me an envelope late one night
in which I found printed, mimeographed and what looked like
photocopies of various illegal publications. One was called
Unidad and was the organ of the Barcelona committee of the

P.S.U.C. If P.S.U.C. meant the same as it had during the war, it meant Unified Socialist Party of Catalonia.

Another was a leaflet issued by the same party, headed DOWN WITH FASCIST REPRESSION! There were also three copies of nothing less than *Mundo Obrero*, organ of the central committee of the Communist Party of Spain, dated from June, September and October of that year. It was a bimonthly that came out on the first and fifteenth of each month, ran to four pages printed on each side and cost a *peseta*.

There was an argument, I remember, between Sylviane and a fat fellow named Lázaro, whom I called *El Pagador* because he handed out money once in awhile, and who it appears was the "administrator" of *Pandora*. I thought of him as The Toad because he looked like one, until I saw the Big Boss of the company, who occasionally turned up from Madrid: the producer, whose name was Juan Carlos Victorica. His eyes bulged far more than Lázaro's, so *he* became *El Sapo*. He was always polite when we had occasion to speak, and he seemed distinctly cool, but he could turn a phrase when he cared to. The first time he paid me I said, Thank you, and he said, No, thanks to *you* for your work. (Not much of a phrase at that, is it? but it sounds better in Spanish.)

He wasn't The Boyfriend of The Girlfriend, however. That was a tall and handsome fellow to whom I had said no more than Hello on one or two occasions, and whose name was Manuel Fernández Palacios. He was *always* smiling.

The argument with Lázaro took place over the telephone when he called to say that before we went to Morocco, *Pandora* wanted to sign a contract with me—for the acting job. Sylviane told him that I would sign no contract without the advice of an attorney—then she remembered that Jaime was a lawyer and told Lázaro that if Camino approved of it, I would sign it.

She also asked about the plane ticket and was told it was coming from Madrid. "Why Madrid?" she said. "All you had to do was ask Air France here in town and they could have delivered it."

Apparently that was not the way they did things and Lázaro explained that it was being brought by a man from Madrid that very night—by plane!

Yet it was this same Lázaro who, I was certain, was a fascist, who handed me a brand-new coin when I signed the contract, a handsome silver coin he said was "still rare."

"For good luck," he said and I looked at it. There was The Most General again, gracing a 100-*peseta* piece, and when he handed it to me, Lázaro said, "*Una moneda muy blanda para una cara tan dura.*"

"*Despacio, por favor,*" I said, and he said it slowly: "A very soft money for such a hard face." We laughed.

The contract itself actually called for 40,000 *pesetas* (plus 1,000 a day for expenses) for "interpreting the role of THOMPSON," and was signed between Juan Carlos Victorica, as "*Consejero Delegado de Pandora S.A.,*" (very impressive title, no?) and "Alvah Bessie, actor" (here was *proof!*).

Seven thousand *pesetas* were to be paid on signature; 7,000 at the end of the first week of shooting; 14,000 when I started working again after my return from Morocco; 12,000 on completion of my work. The *dietas* of 1,000 a day were to be paid in advance. (They weren't.)

There was an interesting little codicil which read: "The name of Alvah Bessie cannot appear in the cast, since he is not a professional actor and he is a foreigner."

Sylviane turned up at the hotel to preempt all those *pesetas* (on signature) and went straight to *Air France* and bought one round-trip ticket to Casablanca (for me) and two one-way tickets for each of us. It was her intention to remain in Morocco when I returned for one week to finish "interpreting the role of **THOMPSON**." On my return, we would fly to Paris after Christmas and thence to San Francisco.

On Thursday night at 11:00 Jaime had us picked up by Pipo who drove us to a *tablao flamenco* (that was closed for the season) on the side of Montjuich, and we watched the young María rehearse the dance sequence for the film.

She was good. She was very good indeed in the Andalusian *caña* she performed; her body was under absolutely perfect control; her face displayed those marvelously stylized expressions of *el sentimiento trágico de la vida* that may (or may not) have given Unamuno the title for his classic work; her technique could not have been improved on, nor her training.

I could have understood The Boyfriend's mad passion for her if she had had one spark of the fire that burned in the fat Maruja we had watched with fascination that night in the Plaza Real. (Or even if she had had a few pounds of Maruja's avoirdupois.) She was perfect—and she was cold as ice.

Martita was there (it was cold and raining outside) snapping pictures, The Boyfriend was there, smiling like mad and passing out bottles of excellent *jérz*, and it went on and on while Jaime consulted with Marquitos, his assistant director, with the electricians and his cameraman, Luis Cuadrado, and with a fantastic little fat man who was playing a dancing master. He was not only five feet tall and very fat (and plainly homosexual), he was also crippled (he even called himself *El Cojo*); but he was a fantastic actor and dancer and he was also a dancing master in real life. I was certain he would steal the scene from the *estrella*. (He did.)

It went on past twelve, to one, to two and we grew restless. We asked Jaime when he would be finished (for we had no transportation) and he said, *"Ahora mismo,"* but it never finished and he finally assigned Pipo to take us back to our hotel at three a.m. We could not sleep.

On Friday night the work in the lobby of the *Hotel Ritz*

SPAIN AGAIN: "She was very good indeed . . . but he was . . . fantastic . . ."

was supposed to begin at nine. It started at midnight and all the dress-extras who had been sitting around for hours looked embalmed—as well as bored.

This was one of the final sequences, the departure of Dr. Foster, his wife and Dr. Thompson from Barcelona, after the end of the Congress of Neuro-Surgeons, and it provided the occasion for Thompson, complete with a new *boina* he had bought, his camera and his razor-sharp *navaja*, to "shit" Foster, as my wife occasionally puts it when she forgets she is not speaking French.

The crew and extras and the people hanging around seemed to think this scene was very funny, but after doing it 17 times I could not see what was so funny about it.

We stopped and we had coffee. We started and did it again. We stopped and had beer. We started and did it again after they had changed the lights. We stopped and had gin and tonic. Then we did it all over again. I was exhausted and I said to Jaime, "If I have another heart attack and die, you'll need a lawyer." He laughed and we did close-ups of Mark Stevens looking shitted, of Thompson shitting him.

Some time after midnight Jaime *el Cid* came dancing up to me, a grin on his face. He was waving an airplane ticket. "Here it is," he said.

"Thank you," I said. "Where did it come from?"

"From Madrid—on the 11 o'clock plane. I *said* you'd get it, didn't I?"

"You did. You've said it every day for five weeks."

"*Pues*, now you have it."

At 3:30 the company chauffeur drove me back to the hotel and to my astonishment I found Sylviane awake and sitting up in bed. I waved the ticket at her and she nodded.

"What time does the bus for Perpignan leave tomorrow morning?" I asked and she said, "Eight."

I groaned.

"I'll be glad to get out of here," she said. "I've walked every street in this city and worn out a pair of shoes."

"I know," I said, adding, unnecessarily, "I love it."

"We had a phone call after you left this evening."

"Yes?"

"I was out walking and when I came back there was a message marked *Urgente*, to call a number in Santa Coloma-de-Farnés."

Now I was wide awake. "Señor Turón?" She shook her head.

"The woman we talked to—I didn't get her name. She said she had spoken to the priest but he knew nothing. She spoke to Turón, the man in charge of the cemetery. He did not have a list.

"Then she said she went to the *Juzgado*, whatever that is, of the *Ayuntamiento*, city government, I suppose. They had a record. They said a *Teniente* Aaron Lopoff had died in the hospital there on September 1, 1938. He was 28 years old. They have no record of where he was buried."

"*Juzgado* means courthouse," I said, idiotically. "*Turón* with one r means field mouse. Aaron was 24," I said, and felt tears rise in my eyes.*

---

* We had made some new friends in Barcelona and had told them the story of our search. By odd coincidence they said they had a friend who was a big wheel in Santa Coloma and promised to pursue the search for us. Three months after our return we had a letter saying, "Our friend . . . investigated about the grave at Sta. Coloma . . . without success. The grave was probably a common one and the place is now unknown. The bodies were removed but no one knows what happened to them. I'm sorry . . ." I was puzzled by that phrase, "The bodies were removed . . ." until I remembered that other Brigade men who had visited Spain since the war, and searched out isolated graves of men who had died in action and been buried on the spot, invariably discovered that the local peasants had been caring for these graves for over 20 years, and placed fresh flowers on them regularly.

IV

Leader of Spain by the Grace of God

1

I did not really *want* to go back to Barcelona to finish the "interpretation" but my wife will never believe it. Neither will she believe I was not responsible for what happened *after* I had finished it—but that is *her* problem.

Her return to Morocco was a very sad experience. She had spent most of her youth there and her nostalgia was far more powerful than my nostalgia for Spain—and had a sounder basis.

It was where she had really enjoyed herself, despite years in a Catholic boarding school and training under the nuns in other schools. It was where she had had scores of friends, where she had gone to dances secretly, because her *really macho* father, whose name was Jesús Molla and who had become a French citizen by fighting for the French in the "pacification" of Morocco and against the Germans in World War I, did not approve of such indecent activities.

She had returned to Morocco after the failure of her first marriage to a G.I. who had helped to "liberate" her country, and spent three years working for the U.S. Air Force at its base at Nouasseur, as an interpreter, multilingual secretary and court clerk. Even then, Morocco had been French.

Now it was an Arab country; it was no longer hers. Most of her friends had moved to France and some had died and no relatives remained in Casablanca except an aunt and uncle, a cousin and his wife and son (and her mother, in the cemetery).

She had told me wild and wonderful tales about her native land; you could go swimming in Casablanca *en plein hiver*; in addition to the Atlantic there were luxurious swimming pools built all along the beach that were open all year around. It was so warm that no heating systems had ever needed to be installed in the thick-walled houses that were warm in winter, cool in summer. There had been nightclubs and *thé dansants*, pleasant cafés and coffee houses.

Casablanca, I gather, had been an exciting place when Morocco was a protectorate of the French, unlike Algeria which had been a part of France. Yet the Algerians had fought a long and brutal war, even though they were French citizens, to get rid of those who had conferred that privilege upon them. Morocco became an independent kingdom without a struggle in 1956.

To me, Casablanca was a drag and it was not advisable to kid Sylviane because Humphrey Bogart was nowhere to be found, nor Ingrid Bergman, Paul Henreid nor even Dooley Wilson ("Play it, Sam."), because *Chez Rick* had never existed and the very mention of that Warner Brothers feature film infuriated her, after 24 years. It infuriated me, too, but for another reason. "Rick" was supposed to have been a volunteer in the International Brigades, and when Claude Rains broached him on the subject, he had lisped, "They paid me well." This, one of its screenwriters (Howard Koch) told me, was supposed to be irony but Bogey apparently had not been able to project it.

To me, Casablanca was part provincial French but mostly it was Glendale, California—with Arabs. The Arabs all spoke French, of course; the Ramadan had just begun and you could get no "service" for some hours after sundown because they had fasted all day and were eating to make up for it. Not even poor old Claude Rains in the *képi* of a French police chief could be found, because there *were* no French policemen any more. Only *very* polite Arabs who could not direct you to the French-named street you wanted to find because the names of the streets had also been changed.

I was far more interested in Rabat, Meknès and Fez, which we visited in an Avis-Rent-a-Car.

"We try harder"

There you can see the fascinating remnants of the great sherifian empire founded by the Arabs at the close of the 7th Century, which had ruled all of northwestern Africa and most of the Iberian peninsula. These were really Arab cities and their effect on any decent citizen of almost any democratic country in the world had to be depressing.

For if the French no longer have a colony, the rich Arabs are now exploiting the poor Arabs and the poverty of the *fellahs* in the countryside and the workers in the *medinas* of Meknès and Fez must be comparable to Oriental degradation.

It is unbearable (but true) that you are rapidly forced to "accept" the presence of the filthy and crippled beggars on every street, the children in rags, shoeless, with suppurating eyes, who follow you for blocks on end, their hands outstretched and crying, *"Miskín!"* (which means not only poor but miserable). Either "get used to it" or get out—for you know there is nothing you can do to alleviate their misery. It is impossible to understand how these people manage to stay alive when every *medina* is jammed with hundreds of identical shops (leather, clothing, metal, sandals, food), each of which is selling identical articles and competing with the others.

It was therefore a relief to plunge—as into a nostalgic bath—into the ruins of what was at one time the greatest Roman city of North Africa. Volubilis is near Meknès and went out of existence as a major Roman center (15,000 population) around 285 A.D. Having had a small taste of Roman antiquity in Barcelona and Tarragona, the marvelously preserved and somewhat reconstructed wreckage of the city was profoundly exciting.

It was incredible (to me) to walk on the cobbled streets of this hillside town and see the ruts worn by the Roman chariots! It was deeply moving to look at the mosaics of their swimming pools and baths—exposed to the African sun for centuries, and still brilliantly colored.

The lead plumbing and ceramic pipes that brought hot water and hot air into the baths are still embedded in the standing walls and if the crumbling remnants of the great Arab empire were depressing, for some reason or other these tombstones—like Caracalla's arch of triumph—that recalled the death of an even greater empire, invigorated me and made me want to live forever, in spite of Shelley's "Ozymandias."

2

I had naively expected to be met by Jaime or even by Pipo *el Tipo* when I arrived in Barcelona late Saturday night. The airport was deserted, so I took a cab to the hotel and found a note which said Señor Camino had called, was out of town but would be back that night. I called his number but there was no answer.

There were two other items in my mailbox: a copy of the magazine *Fotogramas* containing an interview with Jaime, which he had promised me; and an unsigned note in a plain envelope that read:

You recall the magazine I told you about. The young man who wrote that article—on which the suppression of the magazine was "justified"—would like to meet you. He will come with me to your room on Monday afternoon at three, if it is convenient.

I did not know whether I wanted to meet the young man. Suppose it *wasn't* convenient—how could I prevent his visit? Of course, I need not be there, which would be the easiest way out. I knew who had told me about the magazine and no doubt he had a telephone number. Or did he? There was no way of knowing if it *was* the young man who had written the controversial article. They might both be *agents provocateurs*. I remembered Sylviane's anger at me for giving the people in Santa Coloma-de-Farnés our name and hotel and thought, You'd better not get yourself involved in something now. Especially when—

Obviously, the publication had incurred the displeasure of the regime on many levels. For one thing, I had been told, in five years there had been no mention in its pages of The Most General! That should have been enough, but there was more.

It had also incurred, I had been told, seven "infractions" of the Press Law in one year; and after the third, its director had been fired. This time, in addition to the three-month suspension, it had been fined the small sum of 250,000 *pesetas* (worth about $3,570 at the time).

The "controversial" article? A well-written and researched piece (with photographs and names) that revealed the extent of unemployment in Barcelona and elsewhere, and the desperate expedients to which these men were put to find any kind of work—or any kind of money.

Its author demonstrated that there existed in Barcelona and other cities what we call "slave markets"—where men hang around and accept any kind of work offered at any kind of price. Those unable to get work often sell their blood for 250 *pesetas* a donation: "I've sold blood four, five and six

LOCATION (Corbera): Luis Cuadrado (second from left), cameraman; Mark Stevens, Jaime Camino, Marquitos (assistant director).

times in a month," said one, "till the other day I fell unconscious. I'm anemic. I've gone two days at a time without a bite to eat. But what am I supposed to do if I can't find work?"

"These days," said another, "men are good for nothing. My wife's got running knees from scrubbing floors so much. She gets up at four in the morning and comes home at night. Thanks to her, we're able to get something to eat. I've run up and down the coast as far as Cape Creus begging for work and come back with empty hands. I've walked to Logroño because they said there was work there and come right back, sleeping under bridges and eating fruit from the fields. I offered to scrub floors and they laughed at me. Imagine it—women get up to 30 *pesetas* an hour for odd jobs and my last job paid me fifteen."

With admirable restraint, I waited till 11 a.m. on Sunday to call Jaime and he suggested I come to lunch at three. "Where have you been?" I asked and he told me they had started to shoot the sequence at Corbera, but "we froze our peanuts." (This is good French slang.)

"You know," I said, "in Casablanca it snowed for the first time in 20 years, they told us. In Fez there was snow on the low Atlas mountains and the hotel heating system went on the blink, so we got out of there as fast as possible."

"Come over and tell us about it," he said, and I said, "How much of what I wrote did you shoot at Corbera?"

"Almost everything."

"*Muy bien*," I said, and went out to look for last night's *Herald-Tribune* from Paris. It had not come.

If he shot it, will it remain in the film? I wondered. I recalled three questions and answers from his interview in *Fotogramas*:

—What do you think of censorship?

—*In time it must disappear*.

—What is your "protest" in relationship to film?

—*The censorship, which has a mortgage on you from the moment you start to think about the screenplay*.

He had been fairly vague about his new film, had not even mentioned its title:

—According to your first two films* it appears that you have a marked predilection for actual situations. Do the screenplays you intend to film in the future lead in the same direction?

---

* *Los Felices 60* (1964), *Mañana Será Otra Día* (1967).

—My next film represents a shift of many degrees in relation to the last. It attacks a theme that, in many ways, can be quite impor- tant for me as well as for the context of the Spanish cinema. It deals with a historical problem, seen from our own times. Each time I become more interested in the daily world of men who get up at eight o'clock to go to work.

While waiting till three o'clock to go to Camino's home, I sat in the bar of the hotel and wondered about him and his place in the Spanish film industry. Could they do anything to him for what he had said about the censorship? Surely, it was innocuous enough—or would have been, as related, for exam- ple, to the censorship over American films that exists in Hol- lywood. In Spain, however, the *Censura* is an arm of the government that is capable not only of cutting a film to ribbons but also of forbidding it to be made or distributed—and perhaps worse.

One of the *avant-garde* film makers I had met in this same bar, the second week we were in town, had shown me a script that had been forbidden. Others had told me that many feet of their finished films had been cut before exhibition was permitted.

What had been deleted, in those cases, was chiefly erotic material, for the majority of the films themselves must have seemed so "far out" that the *Censura* either gave up in disgust or figured, What the hell, if I don't understand it, neither will the audience.

At two of these films, when we attended, large segments of the audience had either walked out or remained to laugh. I told this to one young director and he said, "I don't give a damn if they understand it or not."

They were gentlemen, these young men, and even if they had made allowances for the difficulty I was having discussing abstract concepts in Spanish, and in snatches of French and

English, they must have thought I was naive—or square —beyond all measure.

"My wife," I had told one, "is an intelligent woman, but she did not understand your film at all."

This time he didn't say he didn't give a damn (*being* a gentleman and Sylviane being present), but asked me politely what *I* thought it meant.

"In the most general terms," I said, "it seems to me that it says these things: that life is hard here in Spain; that it's difficult for young people to make a living; that it's even difficult for them, because of the conditions of your life, to have decent relationships with each other. The relationships tend to become exploitative—on both sides."

"You see," he said. "You understand my film."

It occurred to me that Camino's second feature film, which had opened just before we arrived in Spain, said almost exactly the same thing—and had enjoyed excellent reviews. Concerned with two attractive young people who lived by their wits, had no scruples or morals for that matter, it presented a case history in frustration, in the sort of disengagement and "drop out" that we had seen in our own country. All that was lacking, Sylviane and I had thought, was some sense of *why* these things were happening; why they lived by their wits and did not care to work; why the boy would consent to be kept by the girl; why the girl did not scruple to sell her body when other means of bringing in money failed. Self-censorship, what Camino had meant when he spoke of the "mortgage on you" in his interview, could explain this shortcoming, we had felt.

I took another tack. "Do you agree that film is probably the greatest medium of communication men have ever devised?"

"*Claro.*"

"Then, if you have something to communicate and it does not get across to the audience, you have not communicated very well. Is this true?"

"*Posible*," he said. "But I don't make films for the audience."

"You make them for yourself?"

"Of course."

Both these young film-makers, I had been told, were the sons of well-to-do parents who, even though they did not understand what their sons were up to, were flattered by the idea that they were making films and gave them the money to produce them.

One of them suddenly said to me, "I used to be a member of the Communist Party, but I left it some time ago."

"Why?"

"Because the Communist Party here is not interested in making a revolution."

"Is it your opinion," I asked, "that it would be possible to make a revolution in Spain today?"

"You cannot make a revolution without making it."

"But do you think there's a revolutionary *situation* here today?"

"*Claro*," he said.

I was silent for I could scarcely be presumptuous enough to tell a Spaniard about his own country, on the basis of an observation of less than a month. Besides, what he thought of as a revolutionary situation might not correspond with what I thought was a revolutionary situation. Certainly the pot was simmering, even if I did not think that it was boiling.

My silence prompted him to say, "You could have made a socialist revolution here during the war."

"That's what the Trotskyists and the anarchists said."

"They were right."

"Forgive me," I said. "I'm not a Spaniard but I was here

during the war. (I did not add—and *you* had just been born.) "The Spanish people at that time had no interest whatsoever in making a socialist revolution. They wanted to win the war, restore the Republic and improve on it. A majority of the Spanish people had no idea whatsoever what socialism is or stands for or tries to accomplish."

"How many people in Russia," said the other young film director, "were interested in making a socialist revolution in 1917 or knew what it was all about?"

"Very few."

"The October Revolution," he said, "was made by a small minority who knew exactly what it wanted and how to go about getting it."

"True," I said, "but are you comparing Spain in 1936-1939 with Russia in 1917?"

"Obviously."

How do you answer an argument like that? Wasn't the American Revolution made by a minority of activists? In any given revolutionary situation isn't there always a minority that leads the movement, a minority that is in active counter-revolutionary action and a huge, uncommitted mass that is either indifferent or keeps its mouth shut to see which way the wind is blowing?

"I don't think there's any comparison," I said feebly, and the first young man smiled and said, "We disagree."

It was not until later that I remembered what I should have said to these young men, though I doubt they would have been convinced by it: that in addition to the physical differences (population, geography, potential resources, and so forth) between Spain and old Russia, not to mention their respective histories and traditions, there had also been a world war that had lasted four years and killed millions of Russians; that the very same army that, as Lenin put it, had voted for peace "with its feet" by deserting the front, returned to fight both a civil war *and* a war of intervention for five long years when the Revolution so "few" of them understood or knew anything about was in danger.

Walking to Jaime's apartment I was thinking, From active involvement in a revolutionary party, these young men have withdrawn in "disillusionment" so far that now *their* protest is expressed in making films only a handful of people can understand!

I wondered how much satisfaction they got out of it. I wondered, entering Camino's apartment house, how much of the really innocuous dialogue I had written for the Corbera sequence would remain in the film:

SEQ. 37. TOWN IN RUINS. EXT. DAY.

LONG SHOT. David and María are walking through the place. Passing the exposed floor of a destroyed house, in which a window frames the ruins and the countryside beyond it, David walks in.

MARIA: Be careful.

Seen against the light, David moves across the floor until he is inside the window frame, and from that point he dominates the panorama.

DAVID: I was here when it happened.

MARIA: What?

David makes a gesture with one arm, taking in the desolate scene of the destroyed town.

DAVID: All this. . . . Our operating room . . . in a truck . . . was parked outside the town.
        (Ironical expression on his face)
They said it was a military objective. The battalions were at the front . . . about 10 kilometers away.
        (He points)
We came on a Monday night. . . . On Tuesday morning the bombers came over . . . I counted 50. . . .
        (Angry)
There were no more than 30 people in the town itself . . . old men, women, a few children, who had been evacuated . . . but who returned anyhow. . . .
        (Pause)

Twenty minutes later there *was* no town.
                    (Sweeping gesture)
Gone . . . forever.

MARIA (moved):   In wars, many innocent people are killed.

DAVID (looks at her):   Yes. . . .
                    (Turns away, looks at landscape)
After 30 years . . . I can smell the dead buried in the ruins. . . .

3

If you could buy the "social classics" of Marx and Engels openly in Barcelona bookstores (but not those of Lenin,
which are strictly forbidden and can only be found on the black
market), and if you could look at an early (and unimportant)
collection of the notorious Spanish Communist Picasso's work
in a beautiful palace, the only way you can buy books written
from the "wrong" side of the Christian General's *Cruzada* is
under the table. They are few and hard to find and expensive.
You have to be told where to go, and once we had found out,
there were several books I wanted.

I thought it would be best to start with one I had never
seen, which was published in Paris and printed in Switzerland,
was called *Diario de la Guerra de España*, ran to 489 pages in
a large *octavo* with scores of illustrations, and had been written by the Soviet correspondent Mikhail Koltzov, who had
covered the first two years of the war for *Pravda*.

We went to the bookstore and asked the young man in
charge directly for the book, by title and author. He looked up
at us and said, *"Momento,"* went into another room and
closed the door and was gone for almost ten minutes.

When he emerged he said he was very sorry but he did
not have such a book. I asked if it could be found and he said,

"*Posible*," so I gave him our name and address and scrupulously refrained from telling him the name of the person who had recommended his shop.

This had happened the second week we were in town. He had said he would call me when the book came in or deliver it to the hotel, but of course he did not call and did not show. I contemplated giving him the name of my informant, which he had given me permission to do ("if there is any problem"), but decided not to do so.

Instead, we dropped in at the store about once a week and asked for the book each time. Each time he told us that it had not come in. We figured, Forget it, and forgot it. The fourth week we did not ask for it but bought two other books to show goodwill.

The fifth week we were in town, just before we left for Casablanca, a telephone message informed me that the book I had been inquiring for had arrived and we went to the store and received it, already wrapped. It cost 360 *pesetas*, in paperback at that.

Inquiry revealed the fact that other books of a similar nature could be bought: notably, Enrique Lister's *Nuestra Guerra*, the military memoirs of the stonemason who rose to command the Vth Army Corps, Army of the Ebro (published in Paris), and the magnificent autobiography of General Ignacio Hidalgo de Cisnéros (*Cambio de Rumbo*—Change of Course.)

Cisnéros was "a traitor to his class" (the aristocracy). He was one of the few career Spanish air force men to remain loyal to the Republic and he commanded what little aviation the Republic managed to obtain. Characteristically, it was called *La Gloriosa* during the war, and the men of the Lincoln Battalion will never forget the day they made an attack from the top of Hill 666 and had been promised aviation. Five fighters (count 'em, five) roared over our heads and strafed the fascist positions above Gandesa, and were gone. "*La Gloriosa!*" the men shouted and their faces mirrored the letdown we had experienced.

The story of Cisnéros and his equally aristocratic wife, Constancia de la Mora, whose grandfather, Don Antonio Maura, had been prime minister many times under the monarchy, was one of the great personal tragedies of Spain.

Constancia, who served the Republic as chief of its foreign press bureau during the war, was equally a traitor to her class through her loyal adherence to the cause against which the majority of her family and friends were to fight. She had violated Spanish tradition even earlier by going to work for a living and by getting a divorce from her first husband. She told the story in 1939 (*In Place of Splendor*), but the tragedy of the Cisnéros' exile was compounded by the estrangement of the couple in Mexico.

It met its finale in her senseless death in an automobile accident in Guatemala in January, 1950, and in the subsequent frustrated life and death of Ignacio himself. They had been a striking couple—almost archetypes of Spanish beauty, male and female.

He had the long head and the finely structured features you see so often in the paintings of El Greco and Velásquez; she had the dark eyes, the raven hair, the womanly body and the complexion of what Franco likes to call their "race."

Ironically enough, the success of her book in the United States probably sparked their estrangement, for Ignacio was enough of a Spanish male to resent somewhat the attention paid his wife, and in their exile in Mexico there was no way for a career military aviator with no air force to command to make a living. And, at first, he had no other training to equip him for employment—at the age of forty-five.

In *Cambio de Rumbo*, published shortly before his death, Cisnéros gave the lie direct to those who are still saying the Soviet Union either betrayed Spain and/or refused to give it "enough help" to win—and stole its gold reserves, into the bargain.

Sent to the U.S.S.R. by Premier Juan Negrín *after* the withdrawal of all foreign volunteers by the Republic in the late fall of 1938, and with the final fascist drive on Catalonia imminent, he went to Moscow with letters to Stalin, Voroshilov and Kalinin and an urgent request for 250 airplanes, as many tanks, 4,000 machine guns and 650 pieces of artillery.

"These figures," Cisnéros wrote, "seemed prodigious to me. . . . In direct proportion to my enumeration of our needs, I felt more and more embarrassed by the enormity of the figures I was spreading before them. When I had finished, and to my great joy, Stalin gave his consent without blinking an eye. Voroshilov exclaimed, 'Comrade Cisnéros, are you trying to strip us of all our arms?' At the same time, he smiled."

The material requested would cost $103,000,000. "I was shocked," Cisnéros wrote, when Voroshilov asked him how he expected to handle the matter, "not knowing what to say, for the sly Negrín had neglected to tell me that the gold deposited in our Bank of Spain in Moscow was practically exhausted. . . .

"Our Soviet friends exchanged a few words that were not translated for me, consulted some dossiers, then Voroshilov: 'There remains to the credit of the Spanish government, the sum of . . .' (I no longer recall the exact figure, but it did not amount to $100,000.) 'We'll see how we can make up the difference. You can talk about it tomorrow with Comrade Mikoyan, our Minister of Commerce.' . . .

". . . Mikoyan received me in a friendly manner. He had already worked out the form under which our transaction would be handled. The Soviet government agreed to grant a loan to the Spanish government of a sum equivalent to our purchases: my signature alone would guarantee the loan.

"When you think of the often rigorous conditions to which certain governments are obliged to submit to obtain credits, and when you consider beside them the attitude of the U.S.S.R. in advancing, on the sole guarantee of a simple signature and with no collateral whatsoever, more than $100,000,000 to a country at war and on the brink of defeat, you will understand that to speak of disinterest and generosity in this instance is scarcely to use vain words."

Seven ships loaded with the requested material left Murmansk almost immediately. "When the first two reached Bordeaux it would not have been too late if the French government had not put all kinds of spokes in the wheels, and delayed its shipment across France.

"We no longer had any airports available to assemble the airplanes when the convoy finally reached us. In the absence of such a tragic farce, the fate of Cataluña might have been different. We would have had enough material available to resist for several more months. With the state of affairs in Europe at that time, the face of events might have changed.

"We had scores of battalions ready to enter the lines, and we lacked only arms. . . . You can imagine our despair, knowing that masses of *materiél* were immobilized at Bordeaux, while the enemy was advancing. Am I not right when I contend that the French government of that time gave its aid to fascism and contributed to its victory?"*

The subsequent history of Edouard Daladier's government provided the answer to Cisnéros' rhetorical question.

---

* *Virage sur l'Aile* (*Cambio de Rumbo*), Paris: Les Editeurs Français Réunis, 1965.

4

Sunday was pleasantly spent. Jaime and Martita had me
to lunch again at their apartment. They were pleased by the
Christmas presents I had brought from Casablanca—a bottle
of excellent wine grown by people who do not drink alcohol;
the Arab necklace, the notebook for Camino's desk, "bound
in Morocco." Then we went to a projection room to look at
the film that had been shot at the mental institution near Reus.

The young actress who played the *beata* was seated behind me with her mother and her husband, Marquitos, who
was Camino's assistant director. She was as lovely as her
name: Flor de Betania.

Her performance was incredible. I was certain that she
must have seen and studied the young girl who had believed
she was an intellectual, but when I was introduced to her after
the screening (she spoke English, had been born in the
Dominican Republic where her mother had also been an important actress), she said, "No, but Jaime *told* me about her."

"Then how in the world does it happen that I could
almost swear it was the same girl?" She smiled and shrugged.

Her mother suddenly said, "The doctor who is the director of the hospital told Flor that she was just like his patients."

The young actress laughed with embarrassment and I
said, "Under the circumstances, you couldn't want a better
compliment."

"I was worried about the role," Flor said, "until we had
spent an hour or so in the hospital and I noticed that most of
the women were apparently relaxed. So—" she smiled shyly,
"I just relaxed and spoke the lines you wrote for me."

Every genuine work of art always looks as though it had
been easily created, which should be sufficient proof that it
was not. It should also be proof that you *do* have to be an actor
to work in films or on the stage.

At dinner with Jaime and Martita that night, at a restaurant on the Diagonal, he seemed quite unhappy. He said he was not pleased with the way the film was going. I was surprised and referred to the performance by Flor de Betania and he smiled.

"Yes, she's very good," he said. "But she's not the star."

"Ah," I said.

"Yes," said Martita, "you may well say, 'Ah.' "

When I looked at her she said, "Give me an American cigarette, please," and when I lit it for her she coughed deliberately and said, "Too strong for my throat"—which was a line Jaime himself had written for Jacinto, the priest, and was a joke in Spain. (American cigarettes are no longer a novelty and are infinitely milder than the Spanish cigarettes.)

"You should have been an actress yourself," I told her and she shook her head and said, "No. *You* are the actor. And why do you always talk to Jaime and not to me? What are you, anyhow, a *maricón*?"

She was kidding but she was not kidding. She had made that remark several times before. She had commented on the fact that when they had given us a beautiful illustrated book about Spain, I had asked Jaime to sign it first—and then remembered her. "You're always looking at him," she said. "You never look at me."

So I picked up the cue and we played the game for a few moments while Jaime watched us with amusement.

"I would rather look at you," I said, "because you're much prettier. But then Jaime would be jealous."

"You're very *sexy*," she said, using the English word which has now become Spanish, French, Italian, Swedish and every other language in the world.

"I thank you," I said, "but you're too old for me."

"I'm only seventeen."

"Impossible," I said. "You look almost thirty."

"You may be sexy, but you're a *maricón*."

"*Claro*," I said, turning back to Camino, and she said, "You see. You would rather talk to him. How does Sylviane stand it?"

"She doesn't," I said. "Why do you suppose she stayed in Casablanca?"

"She met an Arab," said Martita.

"You saw how bad she was in the *manicomio* sequence," said Jaime, referring to the young María.

It was true. When the director of the institution—who had turned out to be an excellent actor—and Dr. Foster were questioning the young *beata*, María looked as though she were watching a tennis match: her head turned from right to left and back again, without a flicker of any expression appearing on her striking face.

"I would have thought that, as a woman, she would have felt some compassion for those poor women in the institution, and it would have been reflected in her face," I said.

"She's interested only in herself," said Martita. "Just like you and Jaime. You're *both maricónes*."

                                        *

Camino said there would be no work for me on Monday, so I had no reason not to be in my room that afternoon at three o'clock. In fact, on Sunday night when I went back to the hotel, the man who had told me about the magazine was waiting near the elevator and said, "You received my note?"

"Of course."

"It will not be inconvenient?"

"No."

"I will be with him," the man said and I said, "*Muy bien*."

"He's very anxious to meet you. He thinks you're a *maestro*."

"A *what*!?"

"He has read your book, *Los Antinorteamericanos*, and he thinks you're a *maestro*."

What is he, I asked myself, some kind of nut?

He wasn't. Even though he said my novel was the most important he had ever read in his life, he was quite intelligent, very well-informed and seemingly quite rational. Perhaps he had just not read very many novels.

He was also quite personable; 28 years old and, although unemployed, well-dressed.

"Where did you find the book?" I asked, after we had ordered some drinks sent up from the bar and his friend and I had gin and tonics while he drank an orange juice.

"In Burgos prison."

"How did it get there?"

"I don't know," he said. "Books were forbidden there, except, of course, school books and some Catholic material. It could be that the priest brought it in."

"The priest?"

"Does that surprise you?" he said. "You've heard of the Workers' Commissions?"

"Of course."

"Quite frequently they hold their meetings in churches. The priests arrange it."

"But wouldn't the prison authorities have noticed it?"

"They're stupid," he smiled. "But also, the cover was torn off and someone had printed on the fly-leaf, *Gramática Española*."

"You're the second person I've heard of who found that book in Burgos."

"We all read it," he said.

"Excuse me," said his friend. "I will leave now."

We stood and shook hands and when he had left the room I said, "How long were you there?"

"Almost five years."

"You must have been very young."

"I was twenty."

"What were you doing there?" (A stupid question, I told myself.)

"I was associated with a group," the young man said. "We threw a bomb into a police station."

I looked at him amazed. "What did you hope to accomplish by *that*?" (This was another scene out of the Resnais film, *La Guerre Est Finie*.)

"I said before—I was very young."

He insisted on driving me to his home in the suburbs in one of the inevitable *Seats*, and I asked how he could live when he was unemployed.

He said his wife was working; she was a professional. In any event, they had saved some money and he would be back to work on the magazine when it resumed publication after the three-month suspension had ended.

From the suburban house in a new development—a jerry-built affair that looked as though it had started to fall apart as soon as it was finished—we drove back toward Barcelona to pick up their child, who was in school, and I invited them to lunch.

We stopped at a place called *El Quijote* and to my astonishment they ordered the most expensive things on the menu and kept right on ordering. They ordered a very good wine and did not even bother to consult me or ask what I would like to have.

I began a slow burn. Flattery, I thought, is a trap in which ancient and romantic characters can easily be caught. The *cuenta* came to over 1,400 *pesetas*, which was only a little over $20, but for some reason or other it infuriated me.

"Next time," they said, as they dropped me at the hotel, "you must be *our* guest."

"Of course," I said. (*Maestro*, indeed!)*

5

The *maestro* went back to work on Tuesday as an *actor* (it says so in the contract). The sequence to be shot was one of the very first in the film and the conditions surrounding its shooting had made it impossible to complete the work with Dr. Thompson before his interpreter visited Morocco.

For in order to shoot at the Barcelona airport (or any other) you had to have permission from the Ministry of Aviation—and it had taken weeks to obtain. Then there had to be a Pan American jet available and that depended on Pan American's schedule and willingness to cooperate. ("Why not?" said Jaime. "It's a good advertisement for them.")

Now, with this happy concatenation of events—the Ministry's permission, the presence and availability of the Pan Am jet—the sequence would have to be shot that very night because Marianne Koch, the young German actress who was playing Dr. Foster's middle-aged American wife, had to leave

---

* An attempt to locate this young man in 1974 revealed the fact that he had been in prison again and had then been "exiled" to a small town in Catalonia about 150 kilometers from Barcelona. In December 1974 Barbara Probst Solomon, in an article titled "Torture in Spain" in the *New York Times*, revealed that on 16 September 17 prominent Madrid and Barcelona intellectuals had been picked up by the police following the bombing of a Madrid café. Among them were "Lidia Falcón O'Neill, a Barcelona labor lawyer and feminist; her husband, the writer Eliseo Bayo Poblador . . . (etc.) All have been tortured." Lidia is the daughter of César Falcón, prominent Spanish Republican exile and author of a book about the defense of Madrid.

the very next morning for Munich, where she had another film commitment.

We were told that we would start at nine that night and I was transported—again by chauffeured limousine—to the airport. It was freezing cold, just as it had been in Casablanca when I left.

The airport and the city were already decorated for Christmas. In Catholic countries they really do these things up brown and here they were done in excellent taste, for a change.

We did not start at nine o'clock because it seems that they were working on the airplane's engines. It was not a Pan American 707 because the Pan Am jet had suddenly been moved to Madrid, they said, having received word of impending bad weather.

There was an *Iberia Caravelle* in which the sequence would be shot, in first class. There was no Dr. Foster because he had said he would not come to the airport until the scene was lit and ready to be shot. He had told me earlier that he did not mind working ten hours a day, which is the custom in Spain (although it sometimes runs to 12 or 14 hours), but he would be damned if he would work *more* than ten.

At midnight we received word that he would not come at all, since it was too late to start. Pipo was immediately dispatched by Camino to try to change his mind: we could not get another airplane for God knows how long and Marianne Koch *really* had to leave for Munich early in the morning.

It was not Dr. Foster's fault that we didn't start till one in the morning (they were still working on the engines), and he can scarcely be blamed if he turned up fortified against the bone-chilling cold by a supercargo of Spanish vodka.

While we were waiting for him to make an appearance I had time to worry about *Iberia*, for my return flight to Casablanca in three days to spend Christmas *en famille* was aboard two *Iberia* planes. If they worked *that* long on engines ("Only the plane gets more attention than you," their slogan proclaimed), and if their mechanics were anything like the electricians poor Jaime had to contend with in making this film, who knows what would happen?

I was annoyed anyhow because I would have to stay in a hotel in Madrid overnight, en route to Morocco. Oh, there *was* a plane that left Barcelona Saturday morning and connected with a flight to Casablanca, but, as the young lady at *Air France* who had sold us the ticket had said, there was an interval of only 40 minutes in which to change planes.

"How could *Iberia* be 40 minutes late in a one-hour flight?" I had asked her, and she had smiled ambiguously. She *knew* her *Iberia*, which I did not know at the time is considered to be one of the most unreliable airlines in the world. She was a charming young lady named Señorita Figueras, which is the name of the first town in Spain the American volunteers ever saw.

On top of all this, I had been further annoyed—no, *shitted*—by the administrator of *Pandora* in Barcelona, Señor Lázaro, on whom I had called that day at one, by appointment, in the temporary office the firm had rented in the *Hotel Cristal*.

Since I have had a lifelong compulsion to be early for all appointments, I was not justified in being angry when he did not appear at twelve-thirty. When he did not appear at one, I was angry. By the time he did appear, at one-thirty, I was wishing I could swear in Arabic like Sylviane, for he calmly informed me that he did not have the money to pay me.

That chore, he indicated, was to be performed by a third toad whom I had seen around, and who did not put in an appearance for another half-hour. He did not have the money, either, so Lázaro made out a personal check he said I could cash in any bank.

He also refused to pay me in advance, as the contract stipulated, the 6,000 *pesetas* for expenses, saying that after all, I had not worked Monday and would not work Wednesday and since I was leaving Friday night, I was only entitled to the *diarias* for the three days I would work.

He slowly counted out 3,000 *pesetas* from his well-stuffed wallet (*A very soft money for such a hard face*) and my Spanish became even more illiterate as I tried to explain to him that the contract *said* (and I had apparently memorized it without even trying) that the *diarias* were to be paid for every day Señor Betsi was in Barcelona "*a disposición de la película.*"

"I have been here at the disposition of the film since Sunday morning. That makes six days at 1,000 *pesetas* a day, which makes 6,000 *pesetas*."

"*Mi es igual*," he said. "You can take it up with Camino, with Victorica or Palacios."

I said I would. Of course he lied when he said I could cash his check in any bank, and I intended to cash it into dollars. The first bank said, No, it was not the sort of bank that could cash *pesetas* into dollars. It told me to go to a bank around the corner.

The bank around the corner told me it could not cash checks for foreigners, but that I should go to the *Banco de España* on the Plaza de Cataluña, which was a hell of a long way from where I was.

It occurred to me that maybe Lázaro (faithful fellow), Victorica and Palacios were angry about the 40,000 *pesetas* Camino had extracted from them for my role. After all, they had not even wanted to import me in the first place. "How did you do it?" I had asked the director and he said, "Very simple. I said you would not play the part unless you got 40,000 *pesetas*. There is no one else in Spain that we could get. Simple?" "If it was *that* simple," I said, "you should have asked for eighty."

I walked, to let off steam. At the *Banco de España*, after taking a numbered card and waiting half an hour until the number was called, a teller politely informed me that foreigners could not buy dollars with *pesetas*; they could buy *pesetas* with dollars.

"Look," I said, "I'm returning to the United States at the end of this week and I can't *use* 14,000 *pesetas* in the United States."

"You might try to change them at the airport when you leave," this functionary said, "*if* they will cash that many. I do not know."

He gave me the 14,000 *pesetas* and I had to resort to a very dubious expedient to change them into dollars. I got them changed an hour later and I have been hoping ever since that the gentleman who changed them for me did not lose his money or get into any other kind of trouble. (I sent him, at his request, a copy of one of my books, in English, the day we got home and I have never heard another word from him.)

*

It was freezing inside that *Caravelle* in spite of the lights they had rigged up in the first-class cabin, and not the star, the lady playing his wife, the girl playing the Pan Am hostess, the comedy-relief character called Thompson or any of the extras sitting in the seats behind us could wear an overcoat.

We should all have been as warm as the star for we had spent hours in the airport bar, taking aboard cognac and vodka, whiskey and gin and coffee—by installments. But despite this precaution, our breath was visible.

It got to be half-past one and two and half-past two and we did the opening scene over and over. Dr. Foster is looking out the window as we let down to land at Barcelona and Dr. Thompson sits next to him.

THOMPSON: It's amazing. Between Houston and Barcelona there's a difference of seven hours. Actually, according to Greenwich Time, there should only be six.
> (to Hostess)

Miss, what time is it here?

HOSTESS: Eight-thirty, sir.

THOMPSON: You absolutely sure?

HOSTESS (smiling): Yes, Dr. Thompson.

THOMPSON (to David): I think that in countries like this they've got a way of making hours disappear.
> (Looks over David's shoulder out of window)

Man, it's a beautiful city. And mighty large. Has it changed much?

From the window seat there was silence. I looked at the star. He was asleep. Jaime came forward from behind the camera, touched Stevens on the knee and said, "Mark . . . Mark . . . ?"

"Huh?" said Stevens. "Oh yes, where are we?"

THOMPSON: Man, it's a beautiful city. And mighty large. Has it changed much?

DAVID: I suppose. I never saw it from the air.

THOMPSON: When did you see it last?
> (Silence)

CAMINO (coming forward, touching knee): Mark . . . Dabid . . . *por favor.* . . .

STEVENS: What?

THOMPSON: When did you see it last?

DAVID (mumbling): I haven't been back since the war.

THOMPSON: What made you come here in the first place?
> (Silence)

CAMINO (touching knee): Dabid . . . Dabid . . . *por favor.* . . .

6

It was impossible to walk on the Diagonal—which I had privately renamed Avenida del Putisimo—and I walked on it every day, without recalling an event I had never seen.

That was the farewell parade of the International Brigades on that very avenue on 29 October, 1938. It had been preceded by two earlier *despedidas*. First, there was a parade of the entire 35th Division, of which the Lincoln Battalion was a part, which had taken place in the hills between Marsa and Falset on 15 October.

Then there had been the dinner and farewell speeches in Poblet, near Montblanch, three months to the day after we had crossed the Ebro for the first time in our offensive.

At that sad *fiesta* Prime Minister Juan Negrín had spoken; he was forceful, but he seemed very tired. Colonel Modesto, commander of the Army of the Ebro, wept openly when he spoke and it did not seem strange in so positive and masculine a man. Everyone was there: André Marty, who had organized the Brigades and incurred the hatred of more than one man aside from Ernest Hemingway; General Rojo and Enrique Lister; Herbert Matthews of the *New York Times*; Robert Capa, the great photographer of front-line action whose photographer-wife Gerda Taro had been crushed by a tank early in the war and who was to die rather senselessly himself—if somewhat symbolically—in 1954 when he was photographing French troops in North Vietnam. He stepped on an antipersonnel mine laid by the predecessors of the National Liberation Front—the Vietminh—and one of his last comments prefigured what we have done in that wretched land: seeing a French motorcyclist force a group of peasants off the road—by riding close to them—Capa said, "Look at that son-of-a-bitch making new Vietminh!"

I could not get to the last parade in Barcelona because I

was crippled with rheumatism in the town of Ripoll, near the French border, but on October 29th I wrote in my notebook:

The men are back from Barcelona, reporting that the demonstration and parade were worth everything they've been through. Tremendous enthusiasm of the people—women weeping, holding children up to be kissed, girls breaking into the parade to kiss the men. Azaña, Negrín, La Pasionaria reviewed the parade—enormous military display—tanks, artillery, planes diving almost to street level, huge crowds, leaflets dropped over the streets, flags and music.

It must have been Joe Hecht, who survived two years of Spain only to die in his first action in World War II near Saarlautern in Germany (and win a posthumous Silver Star for saving his platoon) who brought me the leaflet I still possess.

It is printed in the red and yellow of the *Generalitat* of Catalonia and is written in Catalan:

> Spain will follow the path to victory,
> which will also be your path!
>
> Spain will tell the world the meaning
> of solidarity among men!

A few weeks earlier Dolores Ibárruri had made the speech from which I quoted earlier:

Mothers! Women! When the years pass by and the wounds of the war are being stanched; when the cloudy memory of the sorrowful, bloody days returns in a present of freedom, peace and wellbeing; when the feelings of rancor are dying away and when pride in a free country is felt equally by all Spaniards, then speak to your children. Tell them of these men of the International Brigades.

Tell them how, coming over seas and mountains, crossing frontiers bristling with bayonets, watched for by raving dogs thirsting to tear at their flesh, these men reached our country as crusaders

JUAN MODESTO: "He did not seem an hour older . . ." (Berlin, 18 July 1961)

for freedom, to fight and die for Spain's liberty and independence. . . . They gave up everything: their loves, their countries, home and fortune; fathers, mothers, wives, brothers, sisters and children, and they came and told us: "We are here. Your cause, Spain's cause, is ours. . . ."

Comrades of the International Brigade: Political reasons, reasons of state, the welfare of that same cause for which you offered your blood with boundless generosity, are sending you back, some of you to your own countries and others to forced exile. You can go proudly. You are history. You are legend. . . .

We shall not forget you, and when the olive tree of peace puts forth its leaves again, entwined with the laurels of the Spanish Republic's victory—come back! . . .

DOLORES (polka-dot dress): ". . . in a small summer cottage . . ." (1961)

I had seen Modesto again—and talked to him—in 1961 when we celebrated the 25th anniversary of the Brigades in East Berlin as guests of the German veterans of the Thael-mann Battalion. He not only spoke at the huge mass meeting and reunion on 18 July in the *Sporthalle*, but he also spoke to the 50-odd American veterans, wives and children in our hotel. He did not seem an hour older than he had looked 23 years earlier. But now he had no home, unless exile in Prague could be called a home.

The woman who had been the greatest tribune of her people throughout the war, had no home either, unless exile in the Soviet Union could be called a home. Walking through the streets of Barcelona and passing what had been the head-quarters of the International Brigade commissariat at Pasaje Mendez Vigo #5 (now the headquarters of an Italian trade organization), it occurred to me that more and more what I had called my home, my native land, was becoming more alien every day.

I had left that same building on the *prensa* truck on September 16, 1938, before dawn, on my way back to Brigade headquarters in the Sierra Caballs. I had been sent back to the Brigade post office in Gratallops seven days later to stop the mail because Negrín had spoken before the League of Nations and announced the immediate withdrawal of all foreign volun-teers from the Republican side—a few hours after the battalion had gone back into action. (We were relieved the next night.)

As I walked the Diagonal I wished with all my heart that I could have Dolores at my side and I thought of her as I had seen her in a small summer cottage about 20 kilometers out of Moscow in August 1961—for the first and what will probably be the last time, unless I get lucky again.

For some reason we will never know, Ernest Heming-way in his *Cosmopolitan* magazine version of the Spanish war, *For Whom the Bell Tolls*, had felt it necessary to slander this great woman—among many other leaders of the Republic.

The slander was not placed in the mouth of his hero, Robert Jordan, who, like his creator, "had no politics," but it was uttered twice: once by a Spanish *guerrillero*, who baited a young Spanish Communist by telling him that Dolores "has a son in Russia since the start of the movement"; the second time by a Soviet correspondent (probably a caricature of

Mikhail Koltzov himself) who referred to her contemptuously as "that great face . . . that great voice."*

*

It is true that Dolores Ibárruri's sole surviving son was sent to the Soviet Union with thousands of other children —and he died there. He is buried in Stalingrad, where he fell with Soviet soldiers under his command, and the small delegation of American veterans of Spain who visited that city in 1961 placed flowers on his tomb. You may find it on the Avenue of Heroes, but you will not notice his name unless you can transliterate the Cyrillic alphabet and read: Rubén Ibárruri. He was 18 when he died in 1942.

His mother, who was in her early seventies in 1961, has lived in the U.S.S.R. ever since the French Republic (*Liberté, Egalité, Fraternité*) made her life in southern France impossible through harassment and the same sort of mindless slander Hemingway had employed.

When we drove out from Moscow to see her on that August 12th we were astounded to meet her walking down the road toward us—a good quarter mile from her cottage.

We piled out of the car and she embraced each of us with powerful arms that nearly cracked our ribs, crying, "*Viejo! Viejo!*" We walked the rest of the way back with her and she served us a lunch she had prepared herself, and we listened as she spoke for 20 minutes without interruption about the situation in Spain, its present and its future.

Her detailed information had astonished us; you would have thought she had a direct pipeline to Madrid or had just returned that afternoon from Barcelona. But it was her confidence in the future of a Spain she had not seen in 22 years that

---

* You will find nothing but affectionate admiration for Dolores in Koltzov's book, *Diario de la Guerra de España*.

moved us even more: This was no sad, bitter, defeated exile such as we have all met from time to time. This was a Spanish woman who had never been separated from her people since she was born in a mud hovel in Vizcaya. That great face may still be seen (for how long?) and that great voice may be heard again in the pages of her autobiography, *El Único Camino (The Only Road)*.*

Road. *Camino*. The making of films. It occurred to me that there was more to be learned about the Spanish war from the great French documentary film that had been put together by Frédéric Rossif, with commentary by Madeleine Chapsal (*Mourir à Madrid—To Die in Madrid*, 1963) than by scores of history books.

It occurred to me that more was said about the continuing struggle in Spain in the French film, *La Guerre Est Finie (The War is Over*, 1966) than you could find (certainly) in either the Spanish press or the great independent and liberal newspapers of the Western world.

Neither film, of course, may be shown in Spain, but the first provoked the regime to make an "answer" called *Vivir a Madrid (To Live in Madrid)* which everyone in Barcelona who had seen it told me was the same thing into which Paco had coverted the *peseta*: *una mierda*.

Film people in Barcelona had seen the two French films in Perpignan and agreed they were remarkable. They had no problem getting there—it could be driven in three hours—and those who had passports went there often to see other foreign films that could not be shown in Spain.

This was just one of the contradictions of living under a dictatorship, just as the showing in Barcelona of such a film as

---

* Published in the United States as *They Shall Not Pass*, New York: International Publishers, 1966.

The Twenty-Fifth Hour (tragicomic in style, anti-Nazi in content), was another. Still another is the fact that the world's most vocally anti-Communist regime is engaged in open and lucrative trade with Communist Cuba and Camino had told me that he had been invited to make a film there himself, and was thinking of going to look around before making up his mind. ("This passport is not valid . . . for travel to or in . . . Albania and Cuba.")

There are those who argue that both *To Die in Madrid* and *The War Is Over* are defeatist. They do not understand the nature of the Spanish struggle. Both are poetic and realistic expressions of the war and its aftermath.

If *To Die* ends on a "downbeat," that is the way the war ended: the Spanish people *were* shoved back into the Middle Ages from which they had emerged only briefly during the eight years of their second Republic. If *The War* conveys the bitterness, weariness and sense of frustration of the Spanish exiles and the couriers who go back and forth from France to Spain to carry propaganda and suggestions from the exiled leadership—it is because they have been doing it for 30 years and they are entitled to be weary, bitter and even frustrated. But they are *not* defeated any more than the people of Spain themselves are defeated—because both of them still maintain the struggle.

People who feel both films are defeatist would not understand the best, most subtle and most Spanish joke about The Most General, who was 75 years old the December we were there:

—I'm giving you a present of a year-old elephant.

—Thank you very much; I can't accept it.

—Why not?

—Because you become very fond of animals, and they die so soon.

7

The swan song of "William Root," the motion picture actor interpreting the role of Dr. Thompson, was sung the next to the last night I was in town, when some scenes from the International Congress of Neuro-Surgeons were shot at the Palacio Nacional on the side of Mountjew.

"Fellini of Spain, I adore you," I said to Jaime before we began work that night. "You've made history with this film, you know."

"How so?"

"I am the only *jeune premier* in the history of the motion picture art who made his debut at the age of sixty-three."

"*Posible*," Jaime said with a wan smile because he was having his own problems.

His problem of course was the young María and how to get her even to *seem* to project something she was incapable of projecting. This is difficult enough with amateur actors even when they have lines to speak, "business" to perform, movements to execute. But the test of any kind of actor comes when he has none of these pieces of equipment to utilize, but must still demonstrate that something is going on inside of him.

The young María merely had to sit in the audience at the Congress of Neuro-Surgeons and listen to what Dr. David Foster was saying from the podium. All she had to go on, as a performer, were the stage directions which read:

María, seated in the audience, listens with a certain air of both surprise and fascination.

(The scene is silent.)

Jaime sat in a row of chairs in front of María and spoke quietly to her. Then he would nod his head as though he had said, "Action! Camera!" and she was supposed to *do* something. Her efforts to do something, I felt, were scarcely assisted by the presence of The Boyfriend, smiling like mad at her from another chair a few rows in front, nodding at her, encouraging her (no doubt) to do her best. Now she seemed incapable of doing anything more than to stare with stupefaction into the middle distance.

Jaime finally gave it up and decided to shoot the entrance into the hall of the Doctors Foster and Thompson. The session had just begun and we spoke no lines as Thompson entered first, moved quietly down the aisle to the second row, then paused and gestured to Dr. Foster to enter the row ahead of him. The two men sat down, put on their headsets that picked up the voices from the simultaneous translation booths in the rear of the hall, and listened.

The stage was quite imposing; there were the flags of all the nations presumably represented at the Congress. There was no flag of the Union of Soviet Socialist Republics, naturally, but neither was there an American flag. (I had noticed this earlier and Marquitos had said they had sent out for one.)

We shot this simple scene in only three takes and from that time on, I was free—and finished. Jaime and Martita had given me two Christmas presents to take back to Casablanca. They insisted that I open mine. It was a magnificent book of photographs of Barcelona and its people and it was so big and heavy we had a fine time joking about how much it would cost in excess baggage charges to take back to the States.

The other package was wrapped but Martita held up a brand-new handbag of handsome leather and said, "It's just like this, except a different color. Since he bought one for Sylviane, I made him buy one just like it for *me*."

Then they both went back to work: Jaime with the male star and members of the audience, Martha taking still photos for future publicity. They had asked me to wait for them so we could eat together. It was midnight then. I said I would and sat wearily in a chair in the reception room outside the hall.

The Boyfriend was smiling all over the place, as usual (The Cheshire Cat?), and handing out bottles of excellent sherry, pouring into paper cups for unoccupied wardrobe and makeup ladies, The Girlfriend, electricians and stagehands, extra players who were not needed at the time.

He approached me with a bottle and cup in hand, gave me the cup and poured into it.

"*Muchas gracias*," I said.

He gestured me into a chair and sat next to me, placing the bottle on a table behind us. Then he looked at me again and said, slowly, "My Ingleesh ees not so good as your Espaneesh."

I shook my head and said, "*Mi español no es tan bueno como tu inglés.*"

Then he just sat and looked at me, smiling and smiling (that swallowed the canary?), and finally and in his own language, he said what he had been waiting all this time to say.

"You have been here before."

"*Perdón?*" I said, although I had understood him perfectly.

"I said, 'You have been here in Spain before.' "

A chill went up my spine despite his smile (*My tables,—meet it is I set it down,/ That one may smile, and smile, and be a villain;/ At least I'm sure it may be so in . . .* in Spain.)

"Whoever told you such a thing?" I said, doing my very best—better than I had ever done for Camino—to capture the Stanislavskian "sense of the object" whatever the hell that meant, and knowing in advance that I had failed.

He laughed. "As a matter of fact," he said, "I knew the moment I saw you wearing a *boina* that you had been here before."

I laughed rather feebly. "Millions of people wear berets," I said. "Not only here and in France, but even in the

United States. I don't like hats. I have no hair. In winter my head gets cold. In summer—"

He was smiling so hard I thought his face would split at any moment.

"You fought at Corbera," he stated flatly and was silent.

"Oh?" I said. There was a long pause.

"I fought at Corbera, too."

This time I was silent and wondered when the *Guardia Civil* would enter the room and how I could communicate my plight to poor Sylviane, trustfully awaiting my arrival in Casablanca for the Christmas dinner.

"On the other side," The Boyfriend added, rather unnecessarily. "*You* were only a sergeant, but I was in command of a battalion—at sixteen."

"You must have been very clever," I said, lamely.

"No," he said. "Just very tall."

Then he got *very* serious and I figured this was the moment the *Guardia Civil* would enter. They didn't. Instead, he said, "It's very good to meet somebody and not have to fight against him."

I couldn't think of anything to reply to that remark, so I was silent. He looked at me carefully and spoke again:

"You forget I approved your contract. I'm wondering why you're working under a false name."

"The contract says my name cannot appear because—"

"No, that's not the reason."

"It's supposed to be a secret," I said idiotically.

"*Porqué?*"

"I don't want the director to get in any trouble. We met in San Francisco and he was good enough to hire me."

That really cracked his face wide open and he shook his head and said, "No trouble for him. No trouble for you, either. After all—it was so long ago."

By this point I had finally realized that there were not

going to be any *Guardia Civil*, nor even a cop or a plainclothes thug, and I was hoping desperately that he was not going to pat me on the head and say, "You poor bastard, we kicked the shit out of you, didn't we? But I can be magnanimous to a gallant foe and even shake your hand."

He didn't shake my hand. Instead, he stood and I automatically stood beside him, looking up into his face, for he is one of the tallest Spaniards I have ever seen.

"You have done very good work on the picture," he said. Then he added, hastily, "Of course, I have not seen the *new* scenes you have written (was there a leer behind those words?), but the acting is very good. You should have credit on the screen."

"*No me importa*," I said.

"I'm serious," he said. "I'll talk to Camino about it."

"It doesn't matter to me," I said again and wondered why I didn't say, I don't *want* my name on the screen. I prefer to remain blacklisted in every country in the world—but certainly and especially in fascist Spain.

"Yes," he said, nodding his head to conclude the conversation. "I will speak to Camino. I think you should have credit for your work—as a writer and an actor."

He picked up the sherry bottle and started across the room to The Girlfriend, who was looking piqued at having been neglected for so long a time.

I felt collapsed. I was suddenly dehydrated and dying of thirst. I was not certain whether I had been humiliated and degraded or merely shown up for a fool and a coward. Shouldn't I have leaped for his throat, screaming, "Fascist pig!" and tried to throttle him? Had I come to this country 29 years ago prepared to die, only to permit myself, like the *peseta*, to be turned into a *mierda* when the enemy himself confronted me? What would I have done if he had actually patted me on the head like a dog or tried to shake my hand?

Does enmity die after 29 years, or 15 or five or one? Do principles evaporate with the passage of time, or in certain circumstances? Or is the enemy not a man but an idea, a concept, an abstraction that cannot be killed whether it wins or loses?

How had I permitted myself to be maneuvered into such a situation? Out of simple vanity? Out of a burning desire to write another moving picture after 20 years on the blacklist? Would I have worked on a moving picture for the chairman of the House Committee on Un-American Activities if he had called me up some day and said he was a film producer now?

Had my return to Spain been "honorable," as Hemingway had put it? Had the opportunity to help make a film that barely touched on what I felt at all—that was essentially innocuous and certainly no threat to the regime—justified my acceptance in advance of the very terms under which it *had* to be made: that it never really deal with the issues?

Many times in the previous weeks I had faced the conflict that raged within me and could not resolve it: on the one hand I felt completely at home with the land and the people (I loved them both); on the other I felt completely alien and a fink, a man who was betraying—by his very presence in this still subjected land, by his acceptance of the coin of the realm, by his daily diet that far surpassed what the Spanish people could afford to eat—that young man of 24 who did or did not lie sleeping in the town cemetery of Santa Coloma-de-Farnés, as well as the 1,800 other Americans who had died in so many other places and the 1,000,000 who had died on both sides to make Spain free or to keep her in bondage.

I could hear Aaron's voice again, saying, "Shit, man, it was almost 30 years ago and you should have forgotten it. It's not *your* fault you didn't die instead of me." (A psychiatrist who had once treated me for severe anxiety had said, "You are a guilty man, you know." "Guilty of *what*?" I had demanded, and he said, "That's what we're trying to find out." We never did.)

I remembered an ancient argument we used to have in Hollywood—an argument that was endemic to the progressive writers there: whether writing for Hollywood was or was not a sell-out of the very ideas we professed to cherish.

That was an easy one to rationalize. We could always claim, with some validity, that our employment at least *prevented* Hollywood from making as many of the vicious antihuman films it so frequently manufactured.

It was a holding action, we used to say, and I could recall several instances in which I had performed such a role on certain scripts. How? By creating real people out of cardboard figures; by supplying genuine motivations for them instead of gimmicks; by attempting to deal with the way people actually live in our world, instead of creating dream situations.

What purpose had it served? Hollywood still continues to manufacture and spread abroad throughout the world its seductive images of sex and violence that are conditioning entire generations to acceptance of a society in which the exploitation of woman by man, the brutalization of man by man, the murder of man by man become as natural as the sunrise.

If *España Otra Vez* (as it would be called at the insistence of the *Censura*, instead of *Spain Again*) did not represent a threat to the regime, neither could it be called pro-fascist, or even reactionary. It reflected one of the contradictions that exist everywhere: made under a fascist regime, it presented a protagonist who had fought against that regime and was neither a renegade nor a repentant. The audience would have to identify with him—if the film were ever shown. If what I had written were retained it would at least point up the man's character and the commitment he had made 30 years before.

I recalled that speech from *La Guerre Est Finie* which suddenly bursts from its hero, the exiled Spaniard Diego, who regularly risks his life slipping into Spain with propaganda designed to help overthrow the regime, and who is tired, disillusioned, almost cynical. (I had met such a man in Hollywood in the 1940's; he had been none of these things, but that was over 20 years ago. We had held a meeting for him in the home of a wealthy businessman—and raised several thousand dollars for him to carry on his work.)

Diego's speech:

Poor, unhappy Spain, heroic Spain. I've had enough of Spain; more than enough. Spain's become the lyrical rallying point of the entire left, a myth for veterans of past wars. Meanwhile, fourteen million tourists go to Spain every year on vacation. All Spain is any more is a tourist's dream, or the myth of the civil war. All of which is mixed up with the theater of Lorca, and I've also had my fill of Lorca's theater: sterile women and rural dramas, who needs them! And that goes for the myth of the civil war, too! I never fought at Verdun, and I wasn't at Teruel either, or at the front at Ebro. And the people who are doing things in Spain today, really important things, weren't there either. They're twenty years old, and it's not our past that makes them militant, it's their own future. Spain isn't the dream of '36 any longer . . . however disturbing that may be. More than thirty years have gone by, and the veterans of past wars give me a pain you know where.

Is this statement defeatist, as some have said? Not at all, for it does not reflect Diego's final action in the film. He returns to Spain on still another dangerous mission. His woman joins the struggle with him. He returns to Spain, thinking of *his* dead comrade, Ramón:

You are going to find Juan, you are going to go with him to Madrid. One last time, you are going to knock at doors, unknown people will open them, you will say something, anything, that the sun is rising over Benidorm, or that the almond trees are in flower in Antonio's garden, and they will ask you in, you will be together, for these are the passwords.

You are going to look at everything with Ramón's eyes, the sky, the vineyards, and the unknown people's faces. You are going to feel all the joy Ramón would have felt, as if this were your first trip, as if the battle were beginning today. . . .*

The Rossif-Chapsal documentary, *Mourir à Madrid*, ends with an elegiac statement, almost a funeral oration over the dead body of the Republic:

NARRATOR: To these starving people they gave a new catechism with their bread:

Question—Are there harmful freedoms?

Response—Yes. Freedom of education, freedom of propaganda, freedom of assembly.

Question—Why are these freedoms harmful?

Response—Because they permit the teaching of error, the propagation of vice and plots against the Church.

NARRATOR: There remained Madrid. Negrín and the Communists wanted to resist unto death. The higher officers of the Republic rebelled. General Casado** formed a "Junta," hoping that between military men a reasonable peace could be obtained. Franco demanded unconditional surrender; they capitulated.

Mussolini wired his congratulations to Franco. Franco wired his gratitude to Mussolini. Franco wired Hitler, saying, "Upon receipt of your congratulations and those of the Ger-

---

* *La Guerre Est Finie*, screenplay by Jorge Semprun for the film by Alain Resnais. New York: Grove Press, Inc. 1967.

** He was actually a colonel.

man nation on the occasion of the final victory of our arms in Madrid, I take the liberty of addressing you with this expression of my gratitude and the gratitude of the Spanish nation, and with the assurance of the friendship of a people who, in the most difficult moments, was able to discover its true friends."

The Narrator calls the roll:

Spain 1939. 503,061 square kilometers—almost as big as France.
There are two million prisoners.
There are 500,000 destroyed houses, one hundred and eighty-three towns seriously devastated.
In three years, one million violent deaths.
Five hundred thousand exiled.
An army of six hundred thousand soldiers.
A single party: the Falange.
A state religion: the Catholic religion.
A single chief-of-state: the Caudillo.
Wages have returned to the level of 1936.
The big landowners got back their land.
The Church got back its vast estates.

That *Caudillo* (by the Grace of God) spoke on December 31, 1939:

What we need is one Spain, united, aware. It is necessary to liquidate the hatred and the passions unleashed by our recent war. But this liquidation must not be accomplished in the liberal manner, with monstrous and baneful amnesties, which are a trick rather than a gesture of pardon.

It must be Christian, thanks to redemption by labor, and it must be accompanied by repentance and by penitence. Anyone who thinks otherwise is either an idiot or a traitor.*

---

* *Mourir à Madrid*. Par Frédéric Rossif et Madeleine Chapsal. Paris: Editions Seghers, 1966.

But the war is *not* over and those who died at Madrid refuse to sleep in their graves. They are the very same people who demonstrate in the streets in every city of Spain these days. They are the students and the workers and even the parish priests who organize daily resistance to the regime and who will reclaim their country in the time to come. They are not repentant; they are not penitent; they have not yet been "redeemed" by 36 years of hard labor.

*

"There is one thing stronger than all the armies in the world," wrote Victor Hugo, "and that is an idea whose time has come." Was that true or false? Hitler's Thousand-Year *Reich* had lasted only 12; Mussolini's neo-Roman Empire, 22; Franco's "One Spain," based on the ideas of Hitler and Mussolini, had already lasted 28 years by 1967.

Fascism, however, is not an *idea*—it is a system. It is what Franklin D. Roosevelt meant when he spoke of "the growth of private power to a point where it becomes stronger than (the) democratic state itself." It is what Dwight David Eisenhower was referring to when he warned about the dangers of a "military-industrial complex" taking over the United States—and how did *that* slip out, or was some subversive speech writer responsible?

It was precisely what Georgi Dimitroff said it was in 1935: ". . . the open, terrorist dictatorship of the most reactionary, most chauvinistic and most imperialist elements of finance capital."

If that sounds like a description of what has started to happen in America these last few years, then make the worst of it. For the mounting opposition of the American people to our criminal war against the people of Vietnam fell on deaf ears for years—until the little men and women in the black pajamas of the National Liberation Front, and their allies, had whipped us to a standstill.

That, alone, plus the division in the ranks of the military-industrial complex, accounted for Lyndon Johnson's offer of 31 March 1968 to "limit" the bombing of the north and accept negotiations looking to end the war. That alone accounted for his "statesmanlike" move toward peace, for the "patriotic" insistence of a bankrupt politician that he would not seek and would not accept the nomination of his party for another term in the White House.

That alone forced the incredible opportunist, Richard Nixon, to campaign for "peace with honor" and contrive a "peace" that cut *our* losses in blood but maintained our profits by letting the Vietnamese fight on with weapons we supply to this very day.

And if *anything* is done to alleviate the desperation of black Americans, only the murder of the Reverend Martin Luther King, Jr., may take credit for it; for until he was shot down in Memphis, Tennessee on 4 April 1968 where he had gone to lead a demonstration of black garbage collectors begging for a decent wage and recognition of their union, the President of the United States himself had ignored the conclusions and recommendations of his own Advisory Commission on Civil Disorders.

Every newspaper had reported that the sale of guns and rifles to private citizens had reached astronomical proportions; that men were being trained from coast to coast in "riot control"; that every major city in the land was stockpiling machine guns, tanks and noxious gases to "contain" the long, hot summer they knew was coming because they would not or could not take any action to prevent it. (Why not? Because, as the Associated Press reported on 7 April: "Johnson is not expected to recommend the far more ambitious and far more costly ghetto improvement proposals put forth in the report of his commission on civil disorders five weeks ago. He has said in the past that Congress would not accept such vast spending in the midst of a war and the prospect of a $20 billion budget deficit.")

Until that climactic and traumatic week in American life, the loathing of our country and what she was doing in the world had only spurred the spokesmen of the military-industrial complex to insist that we would not fail "our commitments," we would not "tuck tail and run," we would "nail that coonskin to the wall" (the word coon has two meanings in the mouth of racist Americans), and we would "stand fast"—until we had wiped out the entire population of Indochina or anyone else who dared oppose our global benevolence.

Perhaps it is no more than a symbol or an omen that before the Reverend Martin Luther King, Jr., was buried, there were insurrections called riots in scores of American cities; there were over 40 dead, 2,000 injured, almost 29,000 arrested (the vast majority of them blacks, of course), and the capital of the United States was garrisoned with twice as many troops as could be found in the besieged American bastion at Khe Sanh in South Vietnam.

8

There had been a sense of impending gloom ever since we were told that the Pan American jet would not be available in which to shoot that opening sequence.

The last day I was in Barcelona, with no work to perform and with all the chickenfeed money finally paid (Camino had spoken to Lázaro), I watched them shoot the sequence in Manuel's bar when Dr. David Foster returns to it for the first time since 1938.

When the lunch break came at four that afternoon, I was

invited to a "farewell party" and there was quite a crowd in the relatively small café. It was the strangest farewell party I have ever attended; nobody but Jaime and Martha paid the slightest attention to the departing guest.

The stars were not there but there was the young actress who played the *beata* and her husband Marquitos. There was the script girl who had originally come from Holland but behaved in a more "Spanish" manner than the Spaniards. There was the young actor-wrestler who played Manuel Jr. and his Gypsy-looking wife. There were the cameraman Luis Cuadrado and his wife, Pipo *el Tipo* and some other people I had never seen before.

We ate and drank and the conversation was general. I could not get one-tenth of it because I have not only been somewhat deaf since Hill 666, but also because no effort was being made to help me understand, by speaking slowly—and why should there have been?

I was remembering that the second night we were in Barcelona, an "omen" had appeared in the form of Mr. Robert Taylor—In Person. The last week I was there, alone, and with Sylviane in Casablanca, another omen appeared in the international edition of the *Herald-Tribune*: a seven-year-old boy had been killed and two other children had been injured when a stunt man lost control of his car during the shooting of a scene from a film called *The Hijackers*.

The star of the film was not involved. His name: Lee J. Cobb, another friendly witness but, unlike Mr. Taylor—for whom I had never cared, even as an actor—Cobb had been one of my closest friends for many years before he decided that expediency was the better part of valor if he wished to remain in the motion-picture industry.

Sandwiched between two friendly witnesses in Spain, stars in their own right and acceptable to all the world, was one unfriendly witness who after 20 years still could not appear under his own name—either as a writer or an "actor."

What was the significance of this? There was none. It is what is called a coincidence; well, two coincidences. Like the fact that I had written the original story for the first picture in which Mark Stevens played a speaking role. Like the fact that at least two people in Spain had read my novel in the Burgos prison. That makes five coincidences. Like the fact that a major sequence in the film was set in Corbera—a town that had been bombed out of existence five hours after we went through it on our way to the front. That the lines I spoke flying over the Pyrenees into Barcelona had been written before I ever spoke them; that one of the owners of the company that made the picture had fought at Corbera too, "on the other side." That of all the screenwriters in America whom Jaime Camino might have met and invited to collaborate with him on a story about an American who had fought in Spain and returned to Spain after 30 years, he had met the *only* American screenwriter who had fought in Spain. He had brought him back to Spain after 29 years and 11 months, knowing nothing of his history when they met.

How many coincidences do you need to create an "omen"? Omen: *Anything perceived or happening that is believed to portend a good or evil event or circumstance in the future; a portent.* What good or evil event was about to happen? Or did I believe would happen? I don't believe in omens, I told myself, and this experience had not convinced me that I had finally broken the blacklist and was about to become an international writer-actor. It was a coincidence, a fluke. Just as it was a coincidence and a fluke that Aaron was probably buried no more than 100 kilometers from Barcelona, but his grave could not be found.

I was staring at the Serrano hams hanging from the ceiling of the café when Jaime said, "What're you looking at?"

I pointed. "Those. Sylviane's mad about them."

"We'll get one as a present," he said, "and you can take it home with you."

"*Prohibido*," I said. "You can't bring it into the country."

"Why not?"

"How should I know?" I said. "It's a fact. Like it's a fact that I can't visit Cuba and you can."

"We may meet next year," Camino said. "We hope to visit Cuba—and Argentina, Martha's home—and Mexico and Hollywood . . . and you."

"That would be nice."

He looked at me and said, "Don't be so sad."

"I'm not."

"You're sad," he said. "You're thinking you will never come back to Spain again."

"I won't."

"Why not?"

"Several reasons. One—I love it here but I hate it. Two—I feel at home and I feel miserable. Three—I'm too old . . . and I'm too broke."

"Now you're not only sad, but you're feeling sorry for yourself."

"*Eso es*."

"It's not *conveniente* for a man like you to be sorry for himself."

"Conquistador!" I said. "I'm of a different time, a different place, a different history." I did not add: I wasn't born in 1936 (like you) but I almost died in 1938. "It's not your fault you didn't," a familiar voice said in my ear. "You don't need to feel guilty about it."

Jaime was saying, "If we get through early enough tonight, I'll drive you to the airport."

"Fine," I said. I knew he wouldn't.

*

It was Pipo who drove me to the airport at ten that night and all the way out I was thinking, I cannot bear to leave this place and I cannot bear to stay. In a sense I really *was* born in this country two years after Jaime and in a sense a good part of me had died here that year. We had not been to half the places I had wanted to revisit; we had not seen one-tenth of what I wanted to see and vainly thought we might see. During the first two weeks Sylviane had said she would like to come back to Spain with me again some time, when we could be tourists, and rent a car again and drive all over the landscape. In Morocco she had said she would never go back to Spain—*or* Morocco.

I had never seen the south, as she had seen it: Málaga, Sevilla, Alicante. I had spent five weeks in Castilla, the balance of 1938 between Aragón and Catalonia. There was Ávila to see, Valencia (in which we had spent only four hours en route to Albacete), Albacete itself and the training base in Tarazona, Córdoba, Almería, Cádiz and Badajoz, Salamanca, Oviedo and the other Basque and Asturian cities, Guadalajara and Toledo and of course, Madrid.

Imagine having fought for the Spain whose beating heart for three long years was in Madrid, and never having seen it! (But you're on your way there now—to spend one night in the Hotel Carlton!)

"I hope to learn a lot about mofie-making," said Pipo, when we were in the airport, "then come to Hollyvood."

"That will be nice," I said.

"If I efer get to Hollyvood," he said, "I vill call you op."

I wrote out our address and our telephone number for him and then the flight was called and he was gone. I was thinking of Jaime's telephone call, as we were leaving the hotel. I hadn't understood half of what he said; he had spoken his rapid Catalan-like French and was trying to say a lot of things at

once and I kept saying, "*No comprendo. Je ne comprends
pas. Plus lentement, s'il te plaît.* Not so *fast!*"

As we boarded the *Iberia Caravelle* I was wondering,
What happens now? If the head of *Pandora*, who said at one
point in that conversation that he had "made some inquiries"
about me, had found out so much, it could not be very long
before the Ministry of Cinematography, or whatever it was,
called in the young director and said, "All right, explain yourself."

"It was one of my follies, bringing you here," he had
told me. "*Pandora* thought that I was crazy."

How much more crazy—or something worse—would the
Ministry think he was, and could they possibly believe so
fantastic a coincidence as this, when I still could not believe it
myself? And would not the identity of his foreign collaborator
practically guarantee that anything I had added to the screenplay would be slashed? If you could not say—in a Spanish
motion picture—that "so many died" during the civil war, if
you could not say "to tell the truth, we all had a hard time after
the war," then could you say what I had written into the
opening scene between the two American doctors, at Corbera,
in the mental institution, in the scene with the priest, Jacinto?

"It's not your fault . . . ." that voice said again. "You
don't need to feel guilty about it." And it added, "And who
the hell do you think *you* are, anyhow?"

*

We came into Madrid's Barajas airport on instruments.
We kept letting down and letting down and letting down until I
was certain we would let ourselves right down into the flanks
of the Guadarrama Mountains that surround the city.

The highway into town was invisible. The bus crawled.
The birds were walking—if they were awake. The next morn-

ing they were certainly awake and they were still walking. I took a cab and then a bus and crawled out to the airport where there was not a single arrival or departure posted although there were hundreds of people waiting to go to Málaga, Mallorca, Barcelona, to Las Palmas in the Canarias, to San Sebastian and Santiago de Compostela, not to mention Lisbon, Paris, London, Istanbul, Athens, Brussels, Johannesburg and Buenos Aires. It was Christmas weekend.

As the hours crawled by the mechanical voice announced, carefully, in two languages, that Flight Number So-and-So to Such-and-Such a place had been indefinitely postponed. After a couple more hours it was definitely canceled.

I struck up a conversation with an obviously American couple (middle-aged) who were hoping to get to Palma de Mallorca to join their teen-age kids for Christmas. The woman was depressed and talked about going back to their apartment in Madrid, which they were fortunate to have with all these flights being canceled. The man, who was deeply tanned, was being very gay and what the hell.

At one point he said to me, "You know, your face is quite familiar," and I gave the standard answer, "I've had it a long time." We both laughed feebly.

He told me he was originally from Los Angeles but now he had homes in Palma, Madrid and Zürich, where he had a business. He said he was an agent, but didn't say what sort of agent he was.

Then he looked at me again and said, "Hollywood. Am I right? You work in Hollywood."

"I used to. Long ago."

"Yeh, yeh," he said. "What did you say was your name?"

"I didn't. Bessie."

"Sure," he said. "Now I remember. I never forget a

face. The investigation—" He turned to his wife who was guarding their piles of gaily wrapped Christmas presents, which obviously included a guitar, and told her about me. She wasn't interested.

By feeling the various packages and going through the tote bags piled next to the bench she had discovered that they had forgotten the meat they were going to take to Palma with them. She insisted it was her husband's fault; he had left it in the refrigerator. "I *told* you not to forget it," she said. "Yeh," he said, "you did."

Then she announced that she was going back to town to get the meat, and she did. Her husband and I suddenly remembered that since we were obviously stranded instead of in flight to Casablanca or Mallorca, *Iberia* must owe us both a lunch.

It did and we had a fine lunch with wine and he said, "That was sure a mess, wasn't it?" He meant the investigation.

"Yes. It was."

"I first came to Europe 15 years ago," he said, "for R.C.A. Then I started up my own business." He got very vehement. "You know," he said, "I wouldn't go back to the States if you *gave* them to me!"

What a strange thing for a successful American businessman to say, I was thinking, a man who has two homes in Spain at that.

"That Hollywood business was the tip-off," he said. "Then McCarthy. Look at what we're doing in Vietnam! We have no business there. I read yesterday that they put Joan Baez in jail! Can you imagine putting a young kid like that in jail for protesting Johnson's rotten little war!"

He didn't want an answer to that question but I was even more puzzled that he could reject an imperialist America—and accept a fascist Spain.

His wife returned from the city before we were finished with our lunch and handed him a large package. "I *told* you you left it in the fridge."

"Sit down and have some lunch," he said.

At 3:00 the fog had lifted slightly and two or three flights were actually announced. At 3:30 the flight to Mallorca was called and my transient friends took off. "Don't worry," he said to me. "We won't let them strand you here."

At 3:35 the flight to Casablanca was canceled, the airport was closed and I joined a mob of other people who were already besieging the *Iberia* desk on the floor below.

They wanted answers to unanswerable questions: Why did the flights for Málaga and Palma leave while the flight to Santiago de Compostela had been canceled? Why did the London flight take off while the flight to Paris did not?

The *Iberia* girls were trying, coolly, to answer questions in Spanish, French, Italian, German and English. They blew their cool. A man standing next to me said, "Are you spikking Spanish pliss?"

"A little," I said. "What can I do for you?"

"If my plane is not flying, I am wanting hotel."

"I'll do my best," I said. "I need one, too. Where were *you* going, brother?"

"*Ysroël*," he said.

When I could finally get one of *Iberia*'s girls to look at me, and answer, she explained that they could not give anyone a room in a hotel. Why not? Because it's not our policy. Look, I said, every airline in the world—if it cannot deliver you to your destination, when you are in transit, will put you up in a hotel until it can."

"*Iberia* cannot," she said. "It's not our fault about the weather. It's not our fault the airport is closed."

"I have a contract with you," I said firmly, "to be delivered to Casablanca."

"We will deliver you," she said.

"When?"

She looked at her timetable and some other papers. She made a phone call. "We have no flight tomorrow, Sunday," she said. "We have no flight on Monday, which is Christmas." She looked at some more papers. "There is no space on any flight to Casablanca until January 6th."

"That's nice," I said. "I'm leaving Paris January *three* for San Francisco."

To hell with it, I thought. I told the man from Israel that he would have to find a hotel for himself, and why. I picked up my bag and started walking. I was hot and sweating. I saw a desk labelled *Hotel Reservations*, told the two young ladies there my problem and they succeeded in getting me back into the Hotel Carlton.

But I didn't go directly to the hotel. I went to *Air France*, which, for some unimaginable reason I had suddenly decided that I loved. (Maybe because of Señorita Figueras.)

The trip to *Air France* actually made it possible for me to see—from the window of the cab—a little of Madrid: the celebrated *Telefónica* building, for example, that used to be hit by fascist shells fired from Mount Garabitas every day during the war; the Calle de Alcalá, a name that had rung like a bell in my head for 30 years or more. But not the Prado, not the Puerta del Sol, not the University City, not the Retiro Park, not the Hotel Florida where Hemingway and the other correspondents used to live.

The *Air France* lady was as charming as all *Air France* young ladies are supposed to be. She also spoke English and she was very sympathetic and after examining endless papers and schedules and holding conversations with a gentleman at another desk, she told me that the best she could do would be to apply my Madrid-Casablanca ticket (plus $44.00) to a Madrid-Paris ticket that would get me to the French capital in the morning—if the planes were flying.

There goes the dinner *en famille*, I thought. Well, perhaps it was just as well. Sylviane had called before I left Barcelona to tell me that the Casablanca airport was closed for runway repairs and I would have to land at Rabat and take a bus. Or, if I preferred, she and her cousin would drive to Rabat and pick me up. I had told her I'd take the bus.

She will never believe this, I thought, any more than I do. A great dinner had been ordered at the swanky Arab restaurant called *Sijilmasa* just out of town on the beach. Everyone would be there: the cousin and his wife and son and father-in-law; the aunt and uncle. It would cost a fortune but they had all been so nice to us and had not permitted us to spend a *dirham*, and lavished us with presents to take home, it would be a ball. Poor Sylviane, I thought.

It later developed that the airport had *not* been closed for repairs at all. It developed, Sylviane told me with a voice crackling with ice, that His Majesty's villa was close to the airport. His Majesty did not *like* the sound of airplanes. So, His Majesty had simply had the airport closed until he left town and *she* was damned if she would go all the way to Rabat to fly to Paris; she would wait—and did—until His Majesty left town.

When I reached the Hotel Carlton again the desk clerk said, "*Otra vez*," and laughed.

"*España otra vez*," I said, and tried to laugh.

The clerk looked puzzled.

"A new movie," I told him. "Coming out next year. Watch for it."

FADE OUT

V

"What's past is prologue . . ."

1

FADE IN

The new movie? It came out the next year—1968. It was sent to Hollywood as Spain's official entry in the Academy Award race for Best Foreign Film, and did not make it. Neither did it find a distributor in the United States.

After we were home I received letters telling me about the struggle between Camino and Boyfriend—Señor Don Manuel Fernández Palacios. With his right hand Palacios was trying to excise almost everything I had contributed to the film. He succeeded, in part. With his left he was insisting that my name appear in the credits "because I understand he's an important American writer and his name will help sell the film in the United States."

It surely wasn't my name nor Mark Stevens' that made *Otra Vez* a success in Spain: it won a 1,000,000-*peseta* prize from the government-controlled National Syndicate of Entertainment (*Espectaculos*) as the Best Spanish Film released in 1968. The 1,000,000 *pesetas* went into the pockets of Palacios, of course. Camino had a hard enough time collecting what they owed him for direction. (To add one more coincidence to all that had come before, the film was distributed in Spain by *InCine*, which has a symbiotic relationship with Warner Brothers whose boss' testimony had helped to blacklist me for over 20 years.)

The Girlfriend? Well, the critics said Manuela Vargas had now been revealed not only as a fantastic *flamenco* dancer, but as a great actress. This shameless and idiotic judgment convinced me that the same situation must obtain in the world

191

of *espectaculos* as occurs among bullfighters: your manager pays your money and you get good reviews.

The Boyfriend? For some reason nobody can explain, the film was never shown in Barcelona, where most of it takes place. For obvious reasons the brand-new film company called *Pandora* had opened its box once—and closed it forever. It never made another film. Created to star Palacios' mistress, when he did not leave his wife and marry Manuela, Manuela left *him* and married someone else.

Camino? For his own company, *Tibidabo*, he has written, produced and directed two more films: *A Winter in Mallorca* and *To Play the Piano Kills. Mallorca* was based on an autobiographical book by George Sand and should have been an international art-house success. The fact that it was not can only be explained by bad promotion and inadequate distribution, for it is a lovely, timely and moving story about the winter of 1837-38 which Sand spent in the abandoned Carthusian monastery of Valldemosa with her two children and her then lover, Frédéric Chopin.

The performances by Lucia Bose of Italy and British actor Christopher Sandford were brilliant and won Best Actress and Best Actor at the IVth International Film Festival in New Delhi. The "legend" alone should have made the film an international hit for it concerned a prematurely liberated woman whose attitudes and behavior would be approved immediately by her contemporary, militant sisters.

Piano was something else: while it exploited a relationship between an older woman and a younger man (for the second time in two films), it represented a disheartening departure for Camino, a former professor of piano himself, which may reflect some of the major frustrations faced by an honest artist in a dishonest society. "Black" in humor and mood, it is an exercise in existentialist pessimism of the most extreme sort and is full of the symbolism in which Spain's two most celebrated film directors, Luis Buñuel and Carlos Saura, like to luxuriate.

In 1971 Jaime visited the United States for the first time, hoping to obtain releases for both *Otra Vez* and *Mallorca*. He didn't succeed. He showed both films in New York, San Francisco and Hollywood where he ran into an old-line producer who has made a number of fairly important, fairly progressive films. This man told Camino that not only did he "love" *Mallorca* and would find a distributor for it, but he definitely wanted Jaime to direct his next film. He said, "You'll hear from me soon." Camino never did. He did hear from the spectacularly built Finnish photographer and was not allowed to sleep all night—again.

The restrictions on the film-maker in Hollywood (craftwise, not sexual) are certainly onerous, but they cannot be compared in kind or in degree to the really stifling bonds placed on artists trying to make a living and say something of value to their fellow men under the putrescent fascist regime of The Most General. If they do not want to go into exile because they love their country and its people and believe they have something to say to both, they either compromise or they go into some other line of work. Either course can ultimately be fatal to the artist.

2

Spain again? Yes, in 1974. When Sylviane and I got there in the spring, it was the same as we had left it seven years before. It had also changed. Things were both better in Spain—and they were worse. They were better for the rich and "better" for the poor. The quotation marks relate to the so-called "trickle-down" theory of economics, which holds that the more conspicuously the rich consume, spend, invest and/or even waste their substance, the more money eventually trickles down into the pockets of the poor. It is impossible to think of this "theory" without recalling any number of films in which the rich drain their champagne and then joyously hurl their glasses into the fireplace. More work for the poor glassmakers, you know.

So, in that sense—that scores of new plastic hotels, apartment houses, motels, "villas," condominiums, bars and restaurants are being thrown up all over the landscape, polluting it, destroying it, obscuring what is left of it from view; that Spain is now the only country in the world that is host every year to more tourists than it has inhabitants (35,560,000 came in 1973); that these invaders leave billions of dollars (over 3 billion in 1973) in various currencies in various hotels, bars and restaurants; that they rent houses, buy villas, patronize whorehouses, apartments and condominiums, scoop up endless *schlock* souvenirs such as cheap guitars, Andalusian hats, full-size and miniature medieval swords and battle-axes, leather *botas* from which they will never drink wine after the first attempt, and endless reproductions in all sizes of Don Quixote and Sancho Panza—in *this* sense more money does drip into the hands of the Spanish working class.

Those responsible for this economic miracle are not only American tourists, multinational corporations, banks and our military—who dominate the nation today in place of the Nazi-Fascist Axis that brought Franco to power—but also more and more West Germans, Dutch and even Japanese (both individual and corporate). So that the two solid (?) rocks on which the economy of the country now rests are: (1) the tourist industry and, (2) the more than 3,000,000 Spaniards working abroad, mostly in Western Europe, who send a good part of their wages home to their families.

The Spanish worker? The legal minimum wage has risen

from the 96 *pesetas* a day of 1967 to 186 (*Ca.* $3.26) but uncontrolled inflation eats up the difference. That means that many workers must still hold down two jobs to make ends meet—or work overtime. They must also make sure that every able-bodied member of the family is a wage earner as well.

Most taxi drivers in the big cities will say *"mal"* if you ask how things are going and almost every one of them will tell you he must work 15 or 16 hours a day to meet the payments on his cab and contribute something to the home.

A typical daily paper, *La Vanguardia Española*, Barcelona, a large-size tabloid, on a typical day (14 May 1974) ran 28 pages of classified advertisements in both diamond and display types, for everything under the sun that can be rented, hired, bought or sold, from farmlands and buildings to certified public accountants and day laborers.

An "authentic professional" comptroller with a command of English is sought by an international organization: 400,000 *pesetas* a year ($7,017). A multilingual secretary with a command of German, English and Spanish who is also a "perfect" typist and takes shorthand will earn $5,263.

On the other hand, girls to sell little machines and forms used in accounting command $150 a month. Most ads for day laborers (*peones*) do not even bother to state a wage, while a waiter is offered $3,400 a year and a "technical engineer" with at least three years' experience in electrical installations will earn between $4,385 and $5,263 net—the same as the secretary above. Apprentices and bellhops are also sought—14 to 16 years old—no wage stated.

Consider the pathetic case of a domestic worker we met. She says she is 20 years old; she has diabetes and has already lost her molars. Her medical bills are high and her mother put her out to work because she could no longer support her.

"Andalucía" holds down two jobs and has no friends because she "has no time" for them and "I like to be alone."

She is less than five feet tall, has the face of a doll and the voice of an eight-year old. She once attempted suicide and a perceptive woman psychiatrist told a well-to-do divorcée about her, and this good woman invited her to live in her apartment.

"Andalucía" writes songs and sings them. Her favorite is called *Soy como soy* (I am what I am). Her only diversion after her daily work is the television. Her daily work includes eight hours in an office where she runs a photocopy machine and is learning filing and typing—7,000 *pesetas* a month ($117), and the apartment. The lady in whose apartment she lives also pays her 1,000 *pesetas* a week ($16.66) for light housekeeping and running errands. She is invariably cheerful, unless she does not see you watching her. She says she hates Spain and cannot wait to save enough money to go "anywhere else in the world."

It is best not to inquire into the earnings of that class of people who still comprise the Spanish majority—the agricultural *peón*. The Republic gave him land for the first time in the life of his family. Franco took it back and restored it to its original owners: the absentee landlords and the Church.

These hardworking people do not figure much in the news of Spanish unrest—most of which comes from the industrial working class, the miners and the students. This unrest is constantly simmering and comes to a boil at least once a year—requiring the regime to put the lid back on and sit on it.

3

The stability of the regime? The last seven years in Spain present a history of unremitting struggle. No month passes without protest demonstrations and meetings broken up by the police (uniformed, plainclothes, *Guardia Civil* and Army) with increasing brutality. There is an open-end series of political trials that are called criminal trials, which are invariably a travesty on justice and where the sentence is known before the "evidence" is even presented. And there is an increasing number of political prisoners who are called common criminals.

Men and women are arrested daily for organizing to ameliorate their lives. They are imprisoned for protesting when their meetings are broken up. They are tortured for standing up for their principles while in prison. Dragnets are laid when individual acts of desperation are committed.

Priests are fined and "sequestered" for leading a workers' demonstration in Bilbao and there is an immediate protest in Barcelona. A hated police chief is killed in San Sebastian, 250 are arrested and the death penalty is invoked for any demonstration of support for the rebels. Simultaneously, the United States and the Franco government open talks aimed at renewing the leases on military, naval and air bases we have held since 1953. (Missile bases, too.) Franco demands more money. The U.S.A. refuses—then gives in.

In a nation where strikes are forbidden, there are more strikes every year. In 1970 there was a devastating subway strike in Madrid and in Granada striking construction workers were fired upon and three were killed. In 1971 10,000 workers in the *Seat* auto factory in Barcelona struck and tried to occupy the plant and many were injured when police attacked with tear gas and tank trucks throwing streams of high pressure water; 1972 was notorious for the murder of five demonstrating shipyard workers and the wounding of 28 more when police in El Ferrol attacked them for protesting the dismissal of six fellow workers.

In August of the same year a maverick voice was suddenly heard when the secretariat of *all* government-controlled unions complained that censorship was damaging Spain's film industry, which had lost $6.6 million in 1971. "One of the problems . . ." the secretariat said, "is the present form of movie censorship . . . [it] uses hackneyed criteria that restrict and limit the commercial development of our pictures." (No mention of artistic development.) Jaime Camino had said the same thing in two courageous interviews in 1967 and 1970.

The crisis in the labor situation arrived in November 1972 when Marcelino Camacho, outstanding leader of the Workers' Commissions, and a comrade named Eduardo Saborido were given 20 years in prison and a priest who had attended a meeting with them was sentenced to nineteen. This was the beginning of the ordeal of The Carabanchel Ten, which climaxed in 1973 with their trial and condemnation on charges of "illegal association with the character of leadership." That is, they had been engaged in activities legal and acceptable in every civilized nation in the world: the organization of free trade unions; the attempted ameliorization of onerous living and working conditions.

The Ten were workers (Carabanchel the name of the Madrid prison in which they were held). Their trial was so clearly a political process designed to demoralize the workers' movement and the anti-Franco opposition that it immediately attracted international attention. So great was the expression of worldwide indignation—from Belgium, France, West Germany, Great Britain, Italy, Poland, Venezuela, Bulgaria, India and Canada (but not from Washington) that the trial was postponed until fall.

Amnesty International, an organization concerned with civil liberties in every country in the world, charged on 27 August 1973 that Spanish authorities use "widespread, regular and brutally unrestricted torture tactics on imprisoned opponents of the Franco regime." The Spanish police denied the charge and called the accusation "defamation" inspired by the

Spanish Communist Party, blandly ignoring 36 pages of documentation the organization had made public.

So closely interrelated are all events in any society that we must consider the Spanish student rebellion and the present situation of the Catholic Church before we reach the climax of this case or the case of the Basque patriots (see below) and the greatest explosion of the past seven years.

The major universities of Spain opened and closed during those seven years like revolving doors, and the police were always just around the corner. In 1968 the students in Madrid were protesting the Vietnam war and the police beat them unmercifully *after* they agreed to come out from behind their barricades and negotiate. In Valencia they were not only objecting to the war *and* the regime—they also demanded free student unions not controlled by the state and protested the right of the police to invade their campus without permission from their deans.

In January 1969 police fired on Madrid University students protesting the "suicide" of a fellow student they were holding. The university was closed; there were mass round-ups; hundreds were jailed; a three-month "state of exception" (emergency) was decreed and the existence of an international conspiracy to subvert the pure Spanish state was of course discovered. The regime expressed its displeasure at foreign news reports of its repressive measures.

Spanish students were not at all quiet during the next two years, and in January 1972 there were major riots on the Madrid campus, 30,000 students were locked out by an exasperated regime, 250 were arrested and others brutalized by the police during four days of speeches and street fighting.

Two years later, in March 1974, their revulsion to what was going on reached its zenith when students in Madrid, Barcelona, Granada, San Sebastian, Zaragoza and Bilbao protested the execution of a 26-year old Catalan anarchist

—Salvador Puig Antich. For the extirpation of this dangerous young man the regime revived a 14th-century instrument called the *garrote vil.* It is an iron collar fitted with a spike which, gradually tightened, eventually cracks the vertebra and severs the spinal cord. His Excellency, Señor Don Pascual Villar Alberto, new Spanish Ambassador to Australia, saw fit to reply to international outrage over that particular barbarity by saying (9 March), "Garroting is a more humane form of executing a criminal than any other way. It is quick, clean, and there is no blood."

4

A great deal of blood has flowed in Spain since The Most General promised, in an interview with the *London News Chronicle* on 29 July 1936, to "save Spain from Marxism at whatever cost."

"Q. That means you would have to shoot half Spain?

"A. I repeat, at whatever cost."

He did not shoot half Spain; merely 400,000 people. But that blood poisoned the land and continues to be symbolized by the bad blood between Franco and one of his former major supporters: the hierarchy of the Spanish Catholic Church.

In 1969 the Church protested the "state of exception" and Franco ended that particular emergency, proudly proclaiming that his government had made 719 arrests and "destroyed" the E.T.A. (Basque freedom organization), the Unified Socialist Party of Catalonia *and* the Workers' Commissions.

By 1970 an influential organization of lay Catholics and clerics called *Opus Dei* (God's Work) had risen to great power in the government. They enjoyed being called technocrats and they effectively replaced Franco's one political "party," the *Falange*. Simultaneously, *El Caudillo* appointed his alter ego, Admiral Luis Carrero Blanco, "vice president." (The Spaniard's annual income was said to barely average $800.00.)

But when preparations were made that year to try 16 Basques for alleged revolutionary activity, the Church was split over what attitude to take toward a trial that was certain to have worldwide repercussions. The defendants had been held for two years on charges of illegal possession of arms, and for the murder of the hated police chief of San Sebastian, Melitan Manzanas. The prosecution was demanding death sentences for six of the defendants and a total of 752 years in prison for the other ten.*

One of the defendants was a priest and he proudly identified himself in court as a member of a secret Basque guerrilla group. There was a wild outburst as the defendants rushed the police, sang the Basque freedom song and the spectators burst into applause and screaming. International observers were present and the court delayed its verdict. Still another state of emergency was declared in anticipation of further trouble. It came.

In the monastery of Montserrat, 30 miles outside Barcelona and perched on a dramatic peak, 300 Spanish artists and intellectuals locked themselves up over the weekend. Knowing that what they had to say would never be printed by Spanish newspapers, they invited the foreign press and issued a proclamation denouncing the court-martial of the Basques, the regime and its oppressive practices.

---

* Margaret Shedd's *A Silence in Bilbao* (Doubleday, 1974) is a brilliant "fictional" recreation of this celebrated case, and the novelist's research and intuition have probably come closer to the way these things are rigged in Spain than any newspaper account of the trial itself.

The entire opposition was now united. It included everybody from the illegal (and therefore nonexistent) Communists to the liberal Catholics. Civil liberties, such as they were, were immediately suspended in order to "cool" the atmosphere, and Carrero Blanco announced that the government was being reorganized and strengthened to meet still another "threat of Communist subversion."

In Burgos the defendants got exactly what the prosecution had demanded: six double (!) death sentences and long jail terms for the rest. Demonstrations broke out all over Spain and Europe. Appeals for clemency arrived from spokesmen for the Italian, Austrian, Danish, Norwegian and Belgian governments—but none from Richard Nixon, who had slipped into town (In Person) on 2 October, been received at El Pardo and slithered out again in the nick of time.

Franco's army supporters were split between the troglodytes who wanted everything to please go back to the time of The Catholic Kings (1479-1504) and the somewhat younger men headed by the equivalent of the Chairman of our Joint Chiefs of Staff, General Manuel Diez Alegría (watch him). They called on Carrero Blanco, got nowhere, and called on Franco, arguing for some mild political reforms and perhaps even the ouster of Blanco himself. Franco played one group against the other.

On 30 December 1970, to demonstrate that he has not been called A Fine Christian Gentleman in vain, Franco commuted to 30 years' imprisonment the death sentences of the condemned. Even his cabinet had been split on the issue. There were widespread strikes immediately and further protests came from East and West Germany, Sweden, Ireland, France, Switzerland and the U.S.S.R.—but not from Richard Nixon.

The imprisoned Basques, however, were jubilant. They told their lawyers that they had been saving wine from their meals for New Year's Eve, but they had drunk it all the night before, not wanting to waste it if they were to be executed the next morning.

What happened inside the councils of the Spanish hierarchy may remain secret for some time, but following the verdict and the commutation which the lick-spittle Spanish press ascribed to Franco's "personal magnanimity" and said was not motivated by international pressure, and following the convocation in November 1971 of another illegal group in Barcelona that called itself "The Assembly of Catalonia," and which demanded the end of the Franco regime and *no* succeeding kingdom, the Church suddenly spoke:

Meeting in December *it apologized to the people of Spain for the role it had played during the Civil War!*

"The fight against present Spanish social structures is necessary," said a special "justice and peace" commission of the Church, "because men cannot be asked to behave with justice if at the same time they are obliged to live under the inhuman weight of unjust systems.

". . . The problem of justice . . . is the most serious affecting our nation. We have often heard that the peace of Spanish society was gained 32 years ago through armed victory but many may not have realized that a long and painful distance separates the existing official peace assured at the end of the civil war from the now so-called peace."

Then, the organization which had warned its parishioners in 1931 and 1936 that to vote liberal was mortal sin, which had blessed Franco's "crusade against anti-Christ" and serviced his firing squads, went on:

"We humbly recognize and ask pardon because we failed at the proper time to be ministers of reconciliation in the midst of our people, divided by a war between brothers. . . ." It continued, saying Spaniards were not sufficiently guaranteed "the right to physical integrity—that is, protection from bodily

or mental torture. . . ." Priests, it said, should not ordinarily
join specific political movements, but they must speak out on
political matters when these affect human rights. "Silence in
such matters makes the Church a guilty accomplice." *Amen.*

5

Franco did not take kindly to this revolutionary statement
but he was in for further shock during the next two years. He
had been arranging for his succession and had built himself a
monstrously vulgar tomb on the measure of—if not in the taste
of—the Pharoahs, called The Valley of the Fallen. He fondly
believed that not only the self-appointed *Caudillo* and his
"Nationalist" dead would sleep therein in peace, but so great
was his magnanimity that he even consented to allow the
"criminals" who had dared oppose him to lie in the same
valley. Their relatives, so far, have resolutely refused to have
their bodies moved.

But to achieve the continuation of the sort of regime you
have pioneered, created and nurtured for decades, you must
not only select, train and develop a successor, but you must
strengthen the regime itself, find staunch friends and grapple
them to your soul with hoops of—well, gold.

His heir: Juan Carlos de Borbón, the *nada* princeling.

His friends: Since 1953, the various administrations of
the United States of America.

These various administrations have poured billions of
American tax dollars into the Spanish dictator's hands, as
bribes, for arms, for quartering troops and other valuable con-
siderations, as the lawyers put it, and for the lease of air,
naval, military and missile bases.

These leases must be renewed regularly and each time Franco has demanded more gold and each time friend U.S.A. has said, No—and then paid through the nose. In 1969 the pact had actually expired and Franco hinted broadly that he would take tough measures if he didn't get what he wanted for allowing us to support him. (That was about the time a solitary male demonstrator in Madrid was sentenced to seven months in jail for carrying a placard reading, "I humbly demand free elections.")

Agreement was finally reached on temporary renewal of our leases, and columnist Drew Pearson hinted there were secret agreements being drawn up. In 1953 and 1963 Franco had been content with a "rental" of $100,000,000 for these real-estate parcels. Now he wanted a five-year agreement and would consent to accept $300,000,000. To show what a fine democratic fellow he was, he also announced an "amnesty" to Spanish Republicans for the 30th anniversary of his victory—but no prisoners were released. Royalists of the faction that supports pretender Juan de Borbón (Juan Carlos' father) demonstrated against Franco.

With 16,000,000 tourists expected, U.S. planes and tanks were Franco's armament at the annual victory parade in 1969. An agreement was reached and our leases were extended for 15 months at a cost of only $175,000,000 to U.S. taxpayers. Our own *Caudillo* permitted American GI's to conduct joint maneuvers with Spanish troops. They practiced suppressing an imaginary "insurrection," according to a copyrighted story in *Newsweek*, by Flora Lewis. The Department of State admitted that such "war games" had been held but "declined to state" whether our country was now committed to help defend Spain—against the Spanish people. (*San Francisco Chronicle & Examiner*, 14 June 1969.)

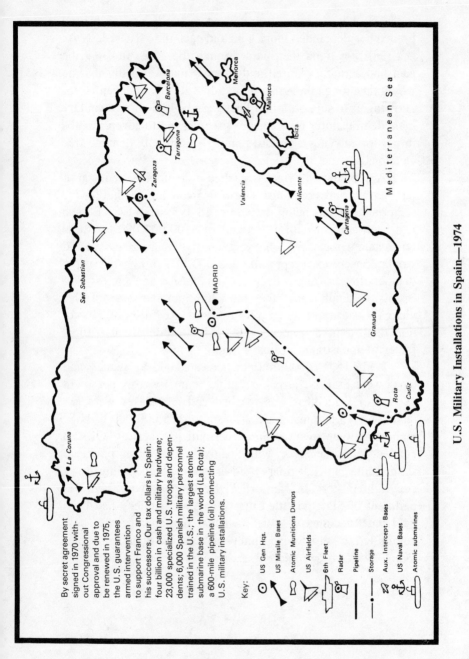

By secret agreement signed in 1970 without Congressional approval and due to be renewed in 1975, the U.S. guarantees armed intervention to support Franco and his successors. Our tax dollars in Spain: four billion in cash and military hardware; 23,000 specialized U.S. troops and dependents; 6,000 Spanish military personnel trained in the U.S.; the largest atomic submarine base in the world (La Rota); a 600-mile pipeline (oil) connecting U.S. military installations.

Key:

Symbol	Description
⊙	US Gen Hqs.
◣	US Missile Bases
◠	Atomic Munitions Dumps
⌂	US Airfields
⛴	6th Fleet
◉	Radar
—	Pipeline
⋯	Storage
✈	Aux. Intercept. Bases
⚓	US Naval Bases
⛴	Atomic submarines

U.S. Military Installations in Spain—1974

Mediterranean Sea

Menorca
Mallorca
Ibiza
Barcelona
Tarragona
Zaragoza
San Sebastian
Valencia
Alicante
Cartagena
MADRID
Granada
Rota
Cadiz
La Coruna

The next month Franco formally appointed Juan Carlos to be the nation's next king. His father, who had been living in Portugal, issued a statement saying he had "reservations and objections" to "the so-called succession law" which was obviously to be enforced "without consulting" him "and the Spanish people's freely expressed will." Spanish newspapers were warned *not* to copy on pain of a fine of $2,143, seizure of the entire edition and other legal consequences. But Don Juan's supporters in Spain demonstrated against The Most General, again.

In 1970 the perennial Franco blackmail operation over "our" bases rose to the surface again and there were indications that this time Nixon would sign a long-term pact as an "executive agreement" rather than as a treaty. A treaty, of course, would have had to be ratified by the Senate. Senator William Fulbright, Chairman of the Foreign Relations Committee, smelled the rat and made loud noises, but then Secretary of Defense Melvin Laird was sent to Madrid to confirm the deal, which was signed and would cost us only $385,000,000 in the next five years.

Twenty-four million tourists had visited Spain in 1970, an increase of 11.2 percent over the previous year. They had left behind $1,700,000,000. But the hunt for more Basques went on and 15 more had been arrested within hours of Franco's "magnanimous" reprieve. His magnanimity did not extend to the *Modelo* (model) prison in Madrid where 70 nonexistent political prisoners began a six-day hunger strike on 28 March 1971, "to protest alleged police brutality and maltreatment by prison authority."

Richard Nixon's *noblesse oblige*, however, was revealed in at least two ways: he rolled out a red carpet and ordered a 19-gun salute to welcome to the *Casa Blanca* the *nada* princeling Juan Carlos, whom he described as "representative of the vibrancy and strength of his people." (*Olé!*) And he sent the chairman of our own Joint Chiefs of Staff, Admiral Thomas Moorer, back to Spain with Juan Carlos and his Greek-born bride, to stand beside Carrero Blanco and celebrate the 32nd anniversary of the destruction of the Spanish Republic at the usual Madrid parade of fascist military might—supplied by us.

Our own admiral was followed by our own Greek-ancestried temporary Vice President Spiro Agnew. He paid an official visit to help celebrate the anniversary of the fascist rebellion on 18 July. He also called on Paco, played a few holes of golf and according to the monarchist sheet, *ABC*, his presence gave the annual fete "special solemnity." The religiously oriented *Ya*, however, disagreed. It permitted a columnist to chide the distinguished guest for his "dangerous oversimplification" of the issues surrounding the Vietnam war and his attacks on the press in America! *Ya* called him "a member of the far right wing." (*Olé!*)

The sirocco was rising again by the end of the year. Rumor had it that American King Ricardo I would like to see Juan Carlos crowned as soon as possible because his patron, The Most General, had fallen asleep twice during Nixon's visit in October 1970.

• A Basque industrialist was kidnapped early in 1972 and held under threat of death by the "destroyed" ETA. He was released unharmed when he agreed to reinstate 183 workers he had fired.

• The cops went to work again on the Madrid students all through January of 1972.

• A civil war memorial in the Basque country was bombed by ETA militants (just as The Valley of the Fallen will be bombed out of existence in the time to come).

• A cop was shot dead in another city in Vizcaya when

four suspected ETA guerrillas were being taken to a police station. They escaped.

 • Nine youths were arrested in Bilbao for distributing "subversive propaganda." There was a gun battle at the French border and two Basques were granted asylum in France while a third was killed.

Franco's 36th year as Spanish "leader by the Grace of God" was celebrated in October and his impending 80th birthday was noted. Also, his intention to remain at his post "as long as" the God whose Grace had placed him there "gives me life and sound judgment." Prince Juan Carlos, the papers said, "was given much exposure at this gala reception in the royal palace" and "remained at Franco's side throughout." (*Olé!*)

Despite this jubilation, inflation was beginning to take its toll, and there was widespread discontent as the cost of living soared. Attempts by the regime to "control profit margins" failed, the *Los Angeles Times* Service reported, and the results of a poll commissioned in 1971 by the government—and then suppressed—became known. It was called the Foessa Poll and sought to determine the political sentiments of the Spanish people. It reported that they were:

 • Communists and Left Socialists—40 percent
 • Christian Democrats—40.5 percent
 • Liberals—13 percent
 • Social Democrats—4 percent

This kind of information, plus the agitation around the case of The Carabanchel Ten, who were being "prepared" for "trial," persuaded Franco to tighten his security a few more notches. The academic charters of three Barcelona universities were suspended, making five such institutions at which emergency (i.e., police) measures were in force.

Franco then appointed his man, Carrero Blanco—said to

be *más Franco que Franco*—Prime Minister. The step was analyzed as a move in the direction of "transference of power" from the failing hands and mind of the 80-year dictator, to his spiritual and physical successors.

Himself 70, Blanco promptly loaded his cabinet with the most hidebound reactionaries in a sharp turn away from what had been described as a centrist-technocrat government. The men who had been doing God's Work (*Opus Dei*, also called God's Octopus) began to be replaced and more was heard from the storm troopers of the reemerging *Falange*, who like to call themselves *Los Guerrilleros de Cristo Rey* (guerrillas of Christ the King—not gorillas).

As preparations for the trial of The Carabanchel Ten went forward, it was announced that in the first six months of the year (1973) Spain had "earned" $1.20 billion from an increase of only 4 percent in the number of tourists over the same period in 1972. The income left by this additional 4 percent added up to a jump of nearly 21 percent in cash money; a better class of tourist, no doubt.

Two alleged Communists were arrested in Barcelona and put away for from six months to six years and on 28 October in the same city, 113 members of the second "Assembly of Catalonia" were arrested in a church and thrown in jail.

Knowing very well indeed who butters his bread, Franco let it be known on 26 November that he would demand nothing less "next time" than a security treaty with the U.S.A. as the price of renewing American military base rights. Said the *New York Times*: "Some officials, particularly in the Pentagon, would be inclined to accept on the ground that a treaty would only formalize an unwritten commitment the U.S. already has to go to the defense of Spain under the existing . . . agreements." Since nobody has threatened Spain within living memory (well, since 1898 when *we* did), the "defense" can only mean the defense of the Franco government against the people of Spain.*

The second week in December (1973) Vincente Cardinal Enrique y Tarancon, Archbishop of Madrid and the loftiest Catholic voice in Spain, called on the government to give Spaniards more political freedom. The loftiest Nixonic voice, Henry Kissinger, called on the *Caudillo* the following week and was scheduled to talk to his foreign minister about negotiations for renewal of the "agreement on friendship and cooperation which covers the 25,000 U.S. servicemen and dependents stationed in Spain."

It was at this nodal point that two explosions took place: one figurative, one literal.

6

Admiral Luis Carrero Blanco was a religious man. (*All* Franco's high-level men, including *El Puto* himself—became *very* religious after they had "won" their war.) The Admiral

---

* On 10 July 1974, the AP reported two items from Madrid: (1) Franco entered a hospital for treatment of phlebitis (another disease he shares with Richard Nixon) and, (2) The Flying Kissinger "initialed" an agreement to "strengthen (the) military ties" between the U.S.A. and Spain and "coordinate them with the Atlantic alliance" (NATO, to which Spain does not belong). It was said we had "three military bases" under a 1970 defense pact in exchange for an estimated $300,000,000 in grants, loans and military equipment." U.S. officials said Spanish officials have "not stated terms for a renewal. Negotiations are to begin shortly." It is good to know that if we are attacked, Franco Spain will come to *our* defense, because as the AP reported, "the defensive ties between the two countries 'must be maintained because their security cannot be disregarded.' " (Kissinger and Cortina.)

had been going to mass every morning at precisely the same time, ever since he was installed as prime minister. He then returned to his car and was driven to his office.

One hour before The Carabanchel Ten's trial opened, the Admiral's car was blown over the roof of the five-story church and landed on a second-story balcony on the other side. The Admiral was in it. So were his chauffeur and a bodyguard.

The lid was clamped on again, but strangely enough the really vicious crackdown that had been expected did not come. (See below, page 220). True, a number of Basques were arrested, six others were named and hunted and the French frontier was closed. A group of four hooded men, announcing they were Basque separatists, held an underground press conference in France and claimed responsibility for the assassination. The French police obliged the Spanish by starting to hunt for them—but could not find them.

Richard Nixon's latent compassion for certain of his fellowmen was finally manifested by the attendance at the Blanco funeral of *his* second handpicked *nada* Vice President, Gerald Ford.

"Prostrated with grief," Franco did not appear. The right wing was encouraged to celebrate a Roman holiday; it shouted from the sidelines, demanding stronger measures against the "Reds," and when the aforementioned Archbishop of Madrid entered the building where Blanco lay in state, part of the crowd called him an assassin and demanded that he be stood up against a wall and shot. (The late Admiral had often clashed with church dignitaries because of their increasing insistence on separation of church and state and their denunciation of the people's lack of freedom.)

The first week of 1974 a new and even tougher cop was installed as prime minister: Carlos Arias Navarro. God's Octopus was said to have been ousted from governmental authority and the *Falange*, Spain's only legal political "party," returned to the government in force.

Arias, infamous for his work as a police security agent between 1957 and 1965, and proud author of the phrase, "the necessity of obedience and discipline," caused some mild surprise in a televised address to the *Cortes*, when he promised that the new regime would permit the existence of political groups—forbidden since 1939. Catch 22a?: Any such groups permitted to exist would be closely screened and must be "entities regulated and recognized by the statute." (*Plus ça change?*)

In view of the touchy situation, it had been felt wise to delay the verdict in the case of The Carabanchel Ten and it had been delayed—one week. As a New Year's present, Marcelino Camacho and Father Eduardo Saborido and the other eight defendants were sentenced to a total of 161 years in prison, and Franco said his former prime minister "had (met) the glorious death every soldier aspires to. He died in the service of his country, in the Grace of God, and with his boots on."

Writing for the *New York Times* (11 January 1974), former U.S. Attorney General Ramsey Clark, who witnessed the trial of The Ten, had this to say:

"No one doubted the outcome . . . [whose defendants] have been sentenced to 12 to 20 years in prison for their labor activities. . . . There was not a shred of evidence introduced that the defendants had even committed the crime for which they were charged. . . . Defying the United Nations Universal Declaration of Human Rights, guarantees which it ratified, Franco Spain denies workers the right to associate, to organize, to hold collective negotiations and to strike."

To nobody's surprise, nothing came of Arias' promise of liberalization, and in February 1974 Monsignor Antonio Anoveros, Archbishop of Bilbao, capital of the Basque country, called in a sermon for greater freedom for his people in running their own affairs.

Franco saw RED. The Archbishop was placed under house arrest and ordered exiled from Spain. He refused to go! Franco appealed to Marcelo Cardinal Gonzales of Toledo, Primate of Spain. The Vatican thereupon shocked Franco further by praising Anoveros' "pastoral dedication." He was summoned to Madrid to talk to the Papal Legate and there was talk that the Spanish Concordat with the Vatican might be breached and terminated.

Support for the embattled prelate was offered following an extraordinary two-day convocation of the Spanish Episcopate, which stated that his expression of sympathy for the Basques did *not* constitute and had not been intended as an attack on national unity. The government discretely agreed to be conciliated and the matter was dropped.

Whereupon Cardinal Archbishop Vincente Enrique y Tarancon promptly defended the Church's right to speak out against social injustice, even if such statements should offend government leaders. "The Church knows," said the most powerful Catholic voice in Spain, "that true liberty and authentic peace cannot be based on injustices. And it does its duty . . . preaching the truth . . . to remind those who govern and those who obey, of their obligations. . . ."

This uproar coincided with—and was aggravated by —the execution by *garrote* of the anarchist youth Salvador Puig Antich (see pages 199-200). Outraged protest demonstrations took place in Barcelona and sympathy demonstrations were held in Rome and Brussels. Universities in five major cities were closed again. Eight thousand taxi drivers went on strike in Barcelona—not over the execution but protesting a nearly 50 percent hike in the price of gasoline, and 12,000 fishermen hit the docks over a *300 percent* increase in the cost of diesel fuel.

In March Franco scored another "coup" against the underground Communists with the arrest of Francisco Romero Martín, a member of the party's central and executive committees who had been working in Madrid for some time. There are two major factions of the party, both underground and in exile: the majority group led by Dolores Ibárruri (*La Pasionaría*) and Santiago Carrillo, its secretary, which opposed the Soviet invasion of Czechoslovakia in 1968, and a minority faction led by General Enrique Lister, who was a divisional commander during the civil war. (Juan Modesto, Commander of the Army of the Ebro, died in Prague in 1969.)

Interviewed in Paris in April, Carrillo strongly implied that the killing of Carrero Blanco had not been done by the Basque ETA, but was probably the work of the ultraright, "as one episode in the struggle among rival factions for the control of Franco's succession. . . . How is it possible," he asked, "that in a house having as its janitor an active member of the Police Department, those responsible for the deed were able through many weeks to 'quietly' dig a tunnel, stretch wiring and prepare the mechanism without detection?

"The murder . . . and the crisis which that has precipitated, solvable least of all by Arias Navarro," Carrillo concluded, "marks the beginning of a most unstable political situation . . . which coincides with the beginning of a worldwide economic crisis whose consequences will have serious repercussions in Spain. Today's simple condition of restiveness may break out into a formidable storm."*

On 25 April 1974, three weeks before Sylviane and I arrived in Spain again, a situation occurred that may help precipitate that storm: In Portugal, which had suffered a fascist

---

* Late in 1974 a book appeared in Spanish called *Operacíon Ogro* (Operation Ogre), written by one "Julen Agirre," with the subtitle: "How and why we executed Carrero Blanco." It is 192 pages long, was published in both Hendaye and Paris by recognized publishing houses sympathetic to the Spanish Republican cause, and consists of documents, narration, photographs and maps designed to prove that it was indeed the E.T.A. that executed the late Spanish "President." It is exceedingly convincing in its exposition, its political line and even in its language, which is Spanish laced with Basque *argot* undertones.

dictatorship for 40 years under Antonio de Oliveira Salazar and Marcello Caetano, a popular general named Antonio Sebastiao Riberiro de Spinola pulled off a nearly bloodless revolution that sent Caetano and his "president" into luxurious exile.

What was even more astonishing was the incredible fact that a military man who had prosecuted the colonial wars in Africa not only overthrew a fascist dictatorship—he restored bourgeois democracy to his people. He abolished censorship; he formed a provisional government from persons of widely differing political viewpoints; he recalled from exile leaders of the socialist and Communist parties; he offered autonomy and granted independence to the colonies his predecessors had held down for 13 years with blood, torture and fire.

Across the border the Franco dictatorship started to shake in its shoes. The 81-year old Franco appeared at a sports rally surrounded by troops; 200 "known" Communists in Madrid were jailed; all street gatherings were banned and right wing organizations were advised to keep their members at home for fear of a provocation that might bring about "a Portugese-type clash" on the sacred soil of Franco's successful crusade.

7

"Dears," Jaime Camino wrote on 27 April 1974, mixing in his newly acquired English, "O.K. *Os espero el 13 Mayo a las* 11:50 a.m., flight B.E.A." The 13th was a Monday. On Saturday he had called us in London to say he could not be at the airport but would be home on Tuesday. He was at the annual film festival in Cannes—on important business.

Barcelona seemed bigger and noisier than ever. Day and night the *Seats* raced up and down the main avenues and side streets as though involved in a perpetual steeple chase. It is amazing that hundreds are not killed in traffic daily, for the drivers seem to have absolutely no regard for each other—or for pedestrians. They cut in and out without signaling, roar through the streets at speeds far in excess of the legal maximum.

More building was going on everywhere; more streets were torn up, were being repaved with ceramic tiles or excavated to permit installation of new sewer pipes, gas pipes and electric lines. Scores of restaurants and bars with American names, scores of American companies with Spanish-sounding names which are subsidiaries of their "mothers" were found on every street. Joan Crawford's *Pepsi-Cola* was beginning to cut into the sales of *Coca-Cola*.

Most prices were outrageously inflated: a bottle of Spanish beer, *Estrella Dorada*, not a bad imitation Pilsner, cost more than it would have in the States; lunch at a restaurant like *Canario de la Garriga*, opposite the *Hotel Ritz*, that uses linen and whose service was courteous and efficient generally cost ten dollars a person with a sherry and a half-bottle of *rioja*. Meals at small working-class restaurants off the Ramblas or down near the port were often just as good and cost less than half as much, which was still exorbitant—on a worker's wages.

Everybody was talking about the Portugese situation except for those who were talking about the latest fiasco of the puritanical governor of Barcelona. He had recently closed all the whorehouses in the city. He gave each of the women 25,000 *pesetas* ($438 and some pennies) and shipped them out of town. He has had as much success curtailing the activities of these "public women" as he has had cracking down on clandestine publications and "secret" meetings of up to 300 people which take place under the nose of his police.

It took less than 24 hours to pick up a copy of the underground publication called *Documentos API* (*Agencia Popular Informativa*). Its issue of 8 May ran ten single-spaced pages of type so small it hurt the eyes, but it was jammed to its narrow margins with information not to be found in any "official" Spanish newspaper.

That issue had reports from Euzkadi (Basque country) about the execution by the ETA of a particularly vicious Civil Guard corporal named Gregorio Posada. Barcelona reported that there might be a general strike to protest the rising cost of living, and a city teacher's strike. An illegal meeting between Basque and Catalan nationalists to coordinate their activities was reported. First reactions to the recent events in Portugal filled a feature article and there was commentary on the arrest of Francisco Romero Martín and two other officials of the Communist Party. It was reprinted from the Party's underground paper, *Mundo Obrero*.

Carrillo, *API* reported, had spoken about the Portugese *coup* over *Radio España Independiente*, a clandestine station, and his speech had been circulated in Barcelona by the Unified Socialist Party of Catalonia:

> As Communists and Spanish democrats, we greet with sympathy the military Movement that has just triumphed in Portugal. [It] will have profound repercussions in Spain. . . . It is a lesson for those who dream that the fascist dictatorship will survive Franco or his enthronement of Juan Carlos as head of state. And if Juan Carlos had a modicum of common sense he would join his father in Estoril (Portugal) without delay and announce that he would accept the national will as expressed in free elections—elections to be held by a Provisional Government of National Reconciliation. . . .

It is doubtful that Juan Carlos or his puppet-masters possess that modicum of common sense, although he is occasionally permitted to make noises like a liberal. For example: he visited Guernica, the Basque town Hitler's bombers destroyed during the war, and praised the Basques for their historic courage!

The front page of *La Vanguardia* (14 May) featured a television speech by the Minister of Finance who blamed the high prices in Spain on the world economic crisis. Had he waited to listen to a statement made by Nixon's about-to-resign Chairman of the Council of Economic Advisers, Herbert Stein, he might have come up with something more ingenious. That arrogant fellow said (CBS' Face the Nation TV program, 7 July) that inflation was the fault of the American people and it would last for years. He also said he would not approve of cutting the citizens' taxes because "we should not be putting $5 or $10 billion into their hands which they'd only go out and spend." *Plus ça change* and *Olé!*

Page three, which is the second the average reader sees, carried two long stories about a man much admired by the fascist government. One story said he was fighting desperately to "conserve the Presidency"—i.e., to hang onto it—and a think piece from New York reported that there were "serious doubts" (among unnamed people) that real justice would be done in the Watergate case. Who might not get a fair trial? The same man, of course.

In the picture section of the paper there was a photograph of King Hussein of Jordan bowing low over the hand of a living corpse called His Excellency, the Chief of State. Only the back of Paco's head and his chicken-neck were visible. We had been told by many people that he suffers from Parkinson's Disease and is growing progressively more feeble, but the papers regularly report that he "looks fit." Both statements could be wishful thinking.

The Barcelona *Tele/eXpres*, which has a reputation for being somewhat liberal, must have given Franco's Foreign Minister Cortina the shivers on 17 May, for its front page showed General, now President, Spinola of Portugal assuming the burdens of his office in the presence of a portion of his cabinet, including Alvaro Cunhal, Communist minister without portfolio and Mario Soares, socialist, *his* Foreign Minister.

The same paper revealed the fact that José Oriol Arau, an attorney who had defended the garrotted militant, Puig Antich, had been arrested. No reason given. A longer story spoke of the consolidation of the new Portugese coalition government and the fact that the people were moving from high emotion to practical action.

There was also an amusing story—played deadpan —concerning a former minister under Carrero Blanco (Julio Rodriguez) who had published a book in which he also claimed that neither the Communists nor the Basque liberation movement had killed the Admiral. Ah, no, he said, it was the Masons. Asked for some evidence, Rodriguez simply said that since he had come to the conclusion that neither the ETA nor the Communists had done the Admiral in, it *must* have been the Freemasons. *Eso es*.

In the next two weeks:

• The 35th anniversary of Franco's victory ("What victory?" said Dr. Thompson before his speech was censored) was celebrated on 26 May and *El Puto* "looked stronger and healthier than at last year's parade, diplomatic observers agreed."

• On 30 May, in accordance with the announcement by the new premier Arias Navarro that he intended to move toward "liberalization" of the regime, the *Cortes* was asked to pass a new law on the election of town mayors (previously appointed by the government). The only liberalization we noticed since our visit in 1967 was the appearance on newsstands of magazines with "soft-core" eroticism: half-dressed girls in mildly aphrodisiac poses. However—the girls on the beach at Castelldefels, south of Barcelona, were wearing startling bikinis the day we had lunch at a restaurant called *Tropical*.

• The International edition of the *Herald-Tribune* (Paris, 31 May) in a signed dispatch by its Madrid correspondent, had a fascinating story. It said that "Moderate senior army officers, led by Lt. Gen. Manuel Diez Alegría, chairman of the politically oriented High General Staff (page 202) were reported to be carefully evaluating the progress of the new Portugese regime to determine how fast Spain should move toward dismantling the dictatorship established by 81-year old Generalisimo Francisco Franco 35 years ago."

Miguel Acoca, the correspondent, went on to say that the moderates had "come to the forefront . . . following the still unsolved assassination of Carrero Blanco. They seized control of the country . . . and blocked attempts by right-wing generals and their sympathizers to unleash a wave of repression and persecution against opponents of the regime. They even contacted exiled Communist leader Santiago Carrillo. . . ."

This story has had no confirmation or follow-up in any paper we have seen, but true or false it points the direction the wind is blowing and what happened later would seem to substantiate it, in some degree.

The same paper on 3 June stated that a poll published in a Spanish magazine called *Cambio 16* showed that a majority of Spaniards "are not content with one-man rule but want to participate in politics." Those who expressed an opinion placed socialism first as an ideological preference.

On the same day another Civil Guard was killed by Basque militants and about a thousand of his comrades started to hunt for the culprits, who were said to have stolen a company payroll worth $233,000.

On 4 June it was announced that for the first time in the

history of government-run television, it *might* broadcast a debate between three candidates running for representative to the *Cortes* from the Balearic Islands.

The tentative new "liberalization" received a sharp setback on 16 June when General Alegría, whom the ultras considered too liberal, was fired as chairman of the joint chiefs of staff, "reportedly because he is similar to Portugal's new president. . . ." (*San Francisco Chronicle & Examiner*)

Within the week official tolerance of a "free" press ended with the seizure of four publications including *Cambio 16*, *Gentlemen* (one of its writers proposed that Spain establish a democratic monarchy) and a new satiric weekly called *Por Favor* (Please) for "offending public morals": it had printed articles unfavorable to reactionaries in power.

*

Jaime Camino finally arrived from Cannes after a long and exhausting drive. His business there was not finished, he had told us on the long-distance phone, and we urged him to stay until it was. No, he said, he wanted to see us and was starting to drive right after lunch and would return to Cannes after we left for France. He sounded grim.

He should have been happy because he had flown to Rome earlier in the year and won Anthony Quinn's agreement to star in his new film, *Spider Web—1945*. Quinn's prestige would be a big international break for Jaime and since the actor is also bilingual, the film could be shot in Spanish and English at the same time.

When he arrived and had slept until three the next afternoon, Jaime told us why he had been in Cannes; it was not to see the festival. It was because the key man in the Spanish censorship was there and Jaime was trying to change his mind about *1945*. For the censorship, whose approval of a script and the completed film means that the producer can recover 15 percent of the total box-office take—up to 6,000,000 *pesetas*, or $100,000 (it used to be 60 percent of the cost of production)—had done more than suggest certain changes in Jaime's new screenplay. It had condemned the script as written.

Before his arrival, Camino's secretary had loaned us a copy, so we immediately understood why our friend seemed so nervous and distracted, despite his cordiality. Few screenwriters or directors familiar with movie censorship in the United States, for example, could possibly have said what was wrong with *1945* from the viewpoint of the Spanish *Censura*. There was no "prurient" material, if you except an opening sequence in a house of assignation whose erotic aspects are immediately overshadowed by a gangster raid with machine guns, in which a man who is an enemy of the character to be played by Quinn is killed.

We have all seen this character (here called Julio) before. We have watched him for decades, as he operated from behind the scenes: a self-made man, rich and ruthless, the complete opportunist. In too many scenes in too many movies he has picked up telephones and told the editor of the local newspaper to "kill that story," and it has been killed. He has mildly indicated to other henchman that certain people who were in his way needed special treatment, and they have received it. He has often had great charm but he is always a son-of-a-bitch who plays both ends against the middle. And he has rarely been so astutely examined as Camino has examined him in *1945*.

Then what was wrong? Why had the censor condemned the screenplay? It *has* to be made in Spain because it is *about* Spain, post-Civil War and World War II Spain, and Julio had played both sides to his advantage during those wars, too. "Hackneyed criteria" or not, the Spanish censorship does not admit that there *are* such characters in Spain: rich, ruthless, dishonest, opportunistic, who do not hesitate to destroy their friends, lovers, rivals or enemies—emotionally, financially and physically, if need be.

All successful businessmen in Spain are good, honest, fine Christian Gentlemen, like *El Puto* himself. And nobody mentions the scandal in which members of his cabinet were involved not too long ago, in which some $200,000,000 in export credits were shuffled around into the "right" hands, like so many cans of beans. (Nobody but the people, of course.) *Eso es*.

Camino would be the first to agree that the struggle in which he is permanently engaged as a film artist of considerable accomplishment and even more potential, must be subordinate to the struggle of his people for a decent life, but he also recognizes that it is inseparable from that struggle.

This struggle never ends. The ferment mounts in intensity from year to year, from month to month, and it may even reach a final nodal point before this book sees print and transform Spain once more—as Portugal and even Greece are being transformed these days—from a fascist dictatorship to a bourgeois—or even socialist—democracy.

History is in no hurry. When heat is removed from water, it turns to ice; when it is added, the water turns to steam. When people grow dissatisfied to the point of desperation, they change things to satisfy themselves. They did it in Spain in 1873; they did it in 1931 and they will do it again. In a land where strikes have been considered treasonable since 1939, there were 811 strikes in 1973 involving 441,042 workers and costing more than 11,000,000 man-hours of work. (Figures from Franco's own "Labor Office.")

The Workers' Commissions are now affiliated with the rebellious students, with the dissident intellectuals and with wider and wider sections of the clergy, and the astonishing thing about the militancy of these students, intellectuals and now the priests—all of whom risk daily arrest, beating, torture, long years of imprisonment and often death itself—is the fact that practically none of them was even born when the civil war "ended" in 1939. And all of them were educated under fascism and have heard nothing from their leaders, their newspapers, magazines, radios, TV programs, movies, employers, teachers and until recently their priests that was *not* in support of the central ideology of the Franco "crusade."

Their militancy comes from struggle in the factory, on the farms, in the shops, offices and classrooms, even in the army. If you cannot get enough to eat without endless grinding labor, you begin to ask questions—of yourself and of others.

The answers to these questions come in time and the implementation of these answers will obviate such minor annoyances as foreign bases on your territory (the U.S.A. had at least 38 in 1972). They will also free Marcelino Camacho, the 16 Basque prisoners, The Carabanchel Ten and all the political prisoners in the prison called Spain.

They will also do away with the decomposing fascist regime, even if it is true that "you become very fond of animals and they die so soon." They will dispose of the putative King, Juan Carlos de Borbón, and if you ask what will happen when Franco dies and is temporarily buried in the fatuous monstrosity called The Valley of the Fallen, people shrug and say, *"Quien sabe?"*

If you ask whether they think the U.S.A. would suppress any Spanish equivalent of the Portugese coup, *they* will ask if the American people would permit such a thing to happen. What would follow such a coup? you ask, a new republic? *Claro*, a republic with a difference. A socialist republic? *Possible*.

One thing is certain: *Mañana Será Otra Dia*. So we cannot say, *Plus ça change* . . . or even in the resigned Spanish manner, *Eso es*. We *can* say:

This Is Not the End

and, *olé!*

POSTSCRIPT

Certainly it was not the end on Bastille Day in 1974 when the previous paragraph was written. Franco had entered a hospital on 9 July with phlebitis. He handed over the reins of government to the *nada* Juan Carlos; then he "recovered" and "returned to work" just in time to enjoy a pronouncement beamed to Madrid by radio on 30 July (from Paris) announcing the formation of a Democratic Junta ready to take over the government at any time.

This Junta is composed of representatives of political groups from right to left, and from many areas of the Spanish land. It embraces monarchists, liberals, representatives of finance and industry, leaders of the Workers' Commissions and the Communist Party of Spain.

It proclaimed that the dictatorship was coming to an end and called on the people of Spain to be ready to make the transition from dictatorship to democracy which, it said, "will not come as a present but will have to be conquered."

It called for a provisional government of reconciliation that will restore to the Spanish people all rights they lost in 1939 when Franco came to power; it advocated absolute and unconditional amnesty for political prisoners, legalization of all political parties without exception, free trade unions, the right to strike and demonstrate, freedom of information, press, radio and television, an independent judiciary, political neutrality of the armed forces, recognition of political integrity for Catalonians, Basques, Gallegos, separation of church and state, popular elections within 12 to 14 months after the restoration of democratic liberties and integration of Spain into the Common Market.

Across the Atlantic, trapped in the intricate web of chicanery, perjury, obstruction of justice, authoritarian arrogance and just plain-and-fancy larceny, *El Puto*'s admirer Richard Nixon on 9 August was forced to resign the office his supporters had bought and paid for twice. So, perhaps for our country and even for Spain, we can say:

This Is the Beginning

San Rafael, California
January 30, 1975